A THEOLOGY OF PREACHING

Abingdon Preacher's Library

A THEOLOGY
OF PREACHING
·
The Dynamics of the Gospel

Richard Lischer

Abingdon Preacher's Library

William D. Thompson, Editor

ABINGDON
Nashville

A THEOLOGY OF PREACHING: THE DYNAMICS OF THE GOSPEL

Library of Congress Cataloging in Publication Data
LISCHER, RICHARD.
    A theology of preaching.
    (Abingdon preacher's library)
    Includes bibliographical references and indexes.
    1. Preaching. I. Title. II. Series.
    BV4211.2.L536   251   81-1470

                    ISBN 0-687-41570-5   AACR2

MANUFACTURED BY THE PARTHENON PRESS AT
NASHVILLE, TENNESSEE, UNITED STATES OF AMERICA

To My Father and Mother

CONTENTS

EDITOR'S FOREWORD

Preaching has captured the attention of increasingly large segments of the American public. Lay parish committees seeking pastoral leadership consistently rank preaching as the most desirable pastoral skill. Seminary courses and clergy conferences on preaching attract participants in larger numbers than ever. Millions of viewers watch television preachers every week.

What is *good* preaching? is the question of both those who hear it and those who do it. Hearers answer that question instinctively, tuning in the preacher who meets their needs, whether in the pulpit of the neighborhood church or on a broadcast. Preachers need to answer more intentionally.

Time was that a good thick book on preaching would do it, or a miscellaneous smattering of thin ones. The time now seems ripe for a different kind of resource—a carefully conceived, tightly edited series of books whose scope covers the homiletical spectrum and whose individual volumes reveal the latest and best thinking about each specialty within the field of preaching. The volumes in the Abingdon Preacher's Library enable the preacher to understand preaching in its historical setting; to examine its biblical and theological underpinnings; to explore its spiritual, relational, and liturgical dimensions; and to develop insights into its craftsmanship.

Designed primarily for use in the seminary classroom, this series will also serve the practicing preacher whose background in homiletics is spotty or out-of-date, or whose preaching needs strengthening in some specific area.

William D. Thompson
Eastern Baptist Theological Seminary
Philadelphia, Pennsylvania

PREFACE

One of the reasons for the scarcity of theologies of preaching is the unresolved question of preaching's status among the theological disciplines. Take away from preaching exegesis and biblical studies, the history of preaching, the encrustations of lore that cling to the pulpit like barnacles on a saltwater scow, systematic theology and its dialogue with secular disciplines, rhetorical skills such as composition, public speaking, and the art of storytelling—and preaching as an independent entity is left with an exceedingly small plot on which to stand. All that remains is a continuity of sounds and gestures whose evanescence defies capture and whose immediate impact and long-term results are virtually immeasurable. To call such an activity *theology* seems almost an affront to the more substantial, morocco-bound theology of the church, and to suggest that such an activity gives coherence and purpose to theology invites none-too-gentle observations on the ineptitude of most modern preaching. Nevertheless, this book proposes a theological function for preaching. A *Theology of Preaching* is actually a theological preface whose aim is to show how theology informs preaching and how preaching, as a kerygmatic, oral, practical activity, informs theology and brings it to its final form of expression. In a more sophisticated undertaking, the author might be tempted to write a theology of "proclamation," by which some mean the singular activity of preaching, but by which most others mean the church's kerygmatic attitude toward itself and the world as evidenced by its liturgy, preaching, sacraments, body of doctrines and traditions, and its social programs. But because this is a practical theology, I retain the word "preaching," by which I mean the event in which one person (or more) addresses others with the gospel. This event is sponsored by the church and usually occurs in the context of corporate worship. The chapters in this theology do not present a variety of topics as much as a carefully chosen succession of perspectives from which to view a single topic: the dynamics of the gospel in the event of preaching. In a theological preface of such modest proportions, certain categories, e.g., the doctrines of the church, the sacraments, the Holy Spirit, are necessarily underdeveloped, and many options have been left unexplored. What is offered represents my own sense of priorities and my own understanding of those things that generate theology, preaching, and a theology of preaching.

It is a joy to write about theology in a community of theologians and seminarians, and I have greatly benefited from my participation in this community of faith and knowledge. But I suspect that whatever passion I have for preaching, and whatever homiletical peculiarities and bad habits go with me, I have acquired during the past eight years of pastoral responsibilities. The congregation has been my theological laboratory, and I am grateful. I have received help and encouragement from several colleagues and friends in school and parish, who have read some of the chapters in manuscript: my thanks are due Professors Gerhard Sauter of Bonn, Richard Thulin of Gettysburg Lutheran Seminary, Dr. William H. Willimon, and my pastors, D. Paul Nelson and Edgar Schambach. Versions of chapter 1 have appeared in *Currents in Theology and Mission* and *Verkündigung und Forschung*, and portions of chapter 2 in *The Christian Century*.

Richard Lischer
Duke Divinity School
Durham, North Carolina

I. PREACHING AS THEOLOGY

Doctrine and life, colors and light, in one
When they combine and mingle . . .
George Herbert
The Windows

Today, most assessments of modern theology have found a common point of departure: the brokenness of theology. Everyone decries the fragmentation of theology—its paralyzing over-specialization, its Babel of terminology, its alienation from the life of the church—but until the pain is great enough, no one does anything about it. Nowhere does this fragmentation impact with greater force and nowhere is the pain felt more deeply than in the church's preaching. Although preaching is central to the life of the church, it has had to struggle continually against its exclusion from the church's self-reflection, its theology. Augustine wrote the first homiletics, but the early church's greatest theologian defined preaching as a matter of expression and devoted most of *On Christian Doctrine* to discussions of the rules of hermeneutics and rhetoric. *On Christian Doctrine* provided the church with a brilliant text-to-sermon manual from which Christian doctrine was strangely absent. Whether seen as a Christianized rhetoric (as in the influential nineteenth-century homiletician, John Broadus), a plain

conduit for the *real* Word of God (as in many Barthian and a few
Lutheran theologians), or as an exercise in speech and communication (as in many seminary curricula), preaching suffers a certain
theological homelessness. It is forever, as one seminary catalogue
enumerates with painful clarity, "Preaching *and*" liturgy, literature,
liberation, dance. . . . Since its relationship to theology is seldom
mentioned, much less seriously analyzed, preaching endures its *de
facto* exclusion quietly, without argument.

THE EXCLUSION OF PREACHING FROM THEOLOGY

Before we explore the possibilities of integrating theology and
preaching, perhaps we need to darken the picture by sketching a few
of the results of preaching's exclusion from theology. The first is a
lack of substance, or what Spurgeon called "treacle" and H. H.
Farmer, "French lacquer preaching." The preacher may present a
charming and literate discourse, but, because the speech does not
emerge from and rearticulate the organizing principles of the
church's life—its theology—because it does not offer the life of God
in Christ, it suffers the same fate as the seed sown on rocky soil. But
in this case, its rootlessness derives from the preacher's rather than
the hearer's lack of depth.

The second result of this exclusion is the lack of coherence. If the
preacher has mastered Freshman Composition, the message may
possess internal coherence, but externally, the sermon does not look
to the rock from which it was hewn. It coheres to nothing. Many
involved in theological education have puzzled at the low level of
transference between the sophisticated skills acquired in the historical and exegetical fields and their simplistic execution in preaching
and other ministry-related areas. Rudolf Bohren makes his point by
way of overstatement when he observes, "However daring a student
may have been in setting up exegetical hypotheses, when it comes to
preaching he proclaims himself a well-tempered churchman, keeps
a remarkable distance from everything modern, sticks anxiously to
what is sleepily correct, and cultivates an acidulous disposition to
legalism."[1] That too many preachers have stalled at the point of

critical theory or technical proficiency is not the fault of higher criticism, at whose door Bohren lays the failure of preaching, although we must note the paucity of biblical scholars who are willing to take responsibility for proclaiming those texts whose ancient meanings they have uncovered. Gerhard von Rad is an exception, and his definition of exegesis exceptional:

> Both scientific exegesis and preaching are interpretation. Interpretation is always appropriation of an intellectual content that is being transmitted to us. No understanding at all is possible without some form of inward appropriation. It would be an illusion to think that we could deal with the transmitted intellectual contents as a foundry worker handles molten ore with long-handled ladles—and thus keep them at a distance from ourselves. Moreover, no understanding is possible unless what is to be interpreted is applied to ourselves, unless it touches us existentially. Therefore there is also no fundamental distinction between exegesis and preaching. Preaching, too, is interpretation only in a different form of speech, in a different confrontation.[2]

If coherence is to be achieved, we need, not only exegetes who take preaching seriously, but preachers who take exegesis seriously, for whom sermon preparation is more than a Saturday's expedition into *The Interpreter's Bible, Proclamation*, or a host of disreputable sermon "services." The coherence we seek, however, lies at a level deeper than the partnership between exegesis and preaching. It springs from the unity and coherence of the gospel itself.

A third result of preaching's exclusion from theology is preaching's loss of authority. The abuse of true authority always produces an abuse of true obedience. Gerhard Ebeling writes, "Theology is necessary because man is by nature a fanatic."[3] We have so thoroughly confused authority with an authoritarianism based on personal charisma, organizational genius, and persuasive public speaking, that responsible Christians hesitate to exercise the authority vested in preaching. The authority of Jesus is a theme that has been usurped by fundamentalist preachers and adopted as the ideology for their empire-building. We think that if we approach preaching in a spirit of dialogue, disclaiming the obligation to move anyone toward anything, the need for authority will vanish. But the importance of authority cuts across all forms and styles of discourse, because true authority comes from the word of the gospel as mediated by the church. Jesus' authority as God's servant was such that he cast out demons, raised the dead, forgave sins, and commissioned a witnessing church. Who he was and what he did were incorporated into the church's understanding of him and of its life and mission. This corporate understanding has, as a whole and in its constituent elements, become authoritative for proclamation, not in the restrictive sense of dogmatic prohibitions, but in the normative and life-giving power of its original intent.

The fourth result of preaching's exclusion from theology is the irrelevance of preaching. But first, theology must answer accusations of its own irrelevance. Many church members are bored or amused by the theological fads, the theologies of: the death of God, secularity, play, hope, liberation, story, which replace each other faster than fashion styles or football coaches. It was theology's perennial faddism that led Barth to compare theology to the universal struggle for existence in which animals furnished with younger teeth and horns kill those older and weaker than themselves. "The American scholarly scene is one of frenetic decadence with the publication of vast numbers of articles and books which fewer and fewer people read. Most scholars no longer address the lived experience of actual people in the churches or society. Instead they address the current questions of their peers in the professional guild."[4] So why, if theology is so important to the church, are so many pastors and laypeople bored by it? The answer is simple: because so much of what has been passing for theology does not draw its life from the gospel and is therefore utterly incapable of transforming lives or teaching and leading the church.

"Doctrine and life," muses the poet. No one writes about the grotesqueries of life more realistically then the novelist Flannery O'Connor. Yet in correspondence with critics and friends she characterizes her work as an exposition of Catholic doctrine centered in the overwhelming reality of the Incarnation. That kind of assessment is only possible for one who has made the transition from doctrine as an object of investigation to doctrine as a condition of human existence in the presence of God. Only the preacher who is rooted (not buried) in the church's constitutive principles, its doctrine, will be free to address the concerns of living people. Such a preacher will not necessarily live on the boundary between two separate spheres of existence, but will learn to interpret existence in all its dimensions as a gift from God. Then, preaching, because it is rooted in those truths that touch humankind at it deepest levels—creation, identity, love, fulfillment, sin, hope, peace, forgiveness—becomes relevant without losing its soul. By this advocacy of doctrine I do not mean to urge upon preachers a *defensor fidei* complex or a self-conscious embrace of the latest movement, which in many quarters seems to be a return to "orthodoxy." The monk who knows he is praying is not praying. The preacher who is convinced of his doctrinal soundness is not doctrinally sound.[5] But one who accepts the doctrines of the church for their truth-value rather than their use-value, thereby returning them their objective and proclamatory nature, may also be taking the first steps toward regaining the ever-elusive relevance of preaching.

WHAT THEOLOGY DOES FOR PREACHING

By theology I mean systematic theology. It strides beyond the arrangement of biblical themes and motifs, but stops short of symbolics. Systematic theology includes the church's *dogmata*, but, in its dialectical relationship to the world, surpasses dogmatics. It is the most inclusive and all-encompassing of the categories named, but it never represents a closed system or a monument on which students, like so many mountain climbers or spelunkers, may pick and chip. Systematic theology's openness to the world corresponds with preaching's worldly concerns, yet both arise only from the gospel and both persist only through the sponsorship of the church. Their relationship poses questions that must be answered.[6]

Gerhard Ebeling insists: 'Theology is necessary in order to make preaching as hard for the preacher as it has to be.'[7] Theology monitors the church's proclamation of the gospel. Indeed, theology only has a job to do because of the nature and task of preaching. If preaching did nothing more than restate the ideas of sacred texts, theology would have nothing to do, and the text-to-sermon manual would speak the final word to preachers. But preachers are charged with *proclaiming the gospel in texts, by means of texts, and in faithfulness to texts.*

Many theologians have recognized theology's function as mediator between exegesis and preaching. Karl Barth calls theology the church's "self-test" by which it measures its language and life. As a reflection on proclamation, theology, as well as the preaching it guides, is judged by a single criterion: its obedience to grace.[8] In the work of Barth's successor, Heinrich Ott, the association of preaching and theology comes closest to absolute identification:

> Dogmatics then may not desire to be anything other than a kind of norm for preaching. As such it may not attempt to change itself into something radically different. In accordance with its essential task, aim and churchly function, it must itself in a certain sense exercise a preaching office. . . . Thus dogmatics for its part can only preach, address, persuade. Dogmatics is a preaching to preachers, a pastoral charge of those who find themselves in a difficult, extreme, readily assailable position of having themselves to proclaim the Word of God.[9]

Gerhard Ebeling also assigns a mediatorial position to theology, but is more successful than Ott in clarifying the almost exclusive use of theology *for* preaching while maintaining the distinction between the two theological disciplines. Whereas Ott tends to say "Preaching is theology" *and* "Theology is preaching," Ebeling agrees only to the former, while qualifying the latter sentence with these words: "Theology consitutes a science, proclamation constitutes the church."[10] Here preaching, as oral, proclamatory, and existential, is radically differentiated from reflective theology and is defined as an event that creates and sustains the life of a community.

Theology makes preaching "hard," in Ebeling's word, by driving the preacher back to the core of Christian doctrine. The church has one doctrine, the *doctrina evangelii*, the gospel, to which other articles are organically joined. Without quibbling over its mandatory and optional elements, we may say that this gospel always speaks in the indicative mood and offers all that God has done in the ministry, death, and resurrection of Jesus Christ. A theology is made evangelical, said P. T. Forsyth, not by its conclusions, but by its principles and the measure in which it does justice to the one creative principle of grace.[11] Theology requires the preacher to relate all the articles of the broader gospel—creation, fall, providence, sanctification, church, eschatology—and all the texts of Scripture to this constitutive core of the Christian faith. This is "hard" because other doctrines, not arising from and unrelated to the gospel, have elbowed their way into the company of *the* doctrine. In addition to these theological options and opinions the preacher is confronted with propaganda, sentiment, and other cultural clutter that all but demand equal time in the pulpit. These theology unceremoniously dumps and prepares the preacher for more serious and constructive work.

As long as the preacher believes that it is possible to move directly from text to sermon, the sermon will be awash with unassimilated and unordered biblical assertions. For the preacher as theologian must discover how, in the words of Melanchthon, "the Gospel opens the door to a correct understanding of the whole Bible."[12] I am not issuing a license for the preacher to ride rough-shod over the particularity of texts or to dogmatize the Bible. I am inviting preachers to understand their task as broader and more demanding than the serial restatement of a pericope's religious ideas. Preaching will ask, Why, in the context of Scripture, the church's teaching, and the contemporary situation, does this word need to be heard? Furthermore, it will seek to order the ideas of the text (many of the standard pericopes are a riot of diversified gospel affirmations) in a way that makes theological sense. How *does* one map a way through providence, election, predestination, justification, and resurrection in Romans 8:28-30? What is the relationship between ethics, worship, and the humiliation/exaltation of Jesus in Philippians 2:1-11? What can we say of the church in light of Peter's confession in Matthew 16? What does the "veil" of II Corinthians 3:13 say about the relationship of the Old and New Testaments? Finally, preaching asks, How does this text relate to the core of the faith? How does it cohere? Thus Luther pressed texts, sometimes demanding more than they had to give, that they might *necessitate* Christ.

Practically speaking, this means standing on the publican's side of the temple, lying on the paralytic's mat, being among those taught in the temple—even if the teacher is only a twelve-year-old. The preacher who relates everything to the center is exercising the theological and biblical disciplines, certainly, but also the personal. For the preacher is claiming an identity as a baptized member of the community of faith. Such a preacher also takes seriously the needs of the members of the congregation, who have built into their spiritual sensibilities, as a kind of law, the yearning to hear that which necessitates Christ.

Another way theology calls preaching back to the gospel is by telling preachers what the gospel is not. It is not law. Theology helps the preacher to discard sub-Christian ideas and to relate Christian ones to their source. It also identifies the biblical and experiential reality known as law. The preacher's theological task is to distinguish law from promise, not to effect a separation of the two, but to restore their original, scriptural relationship so that the law may be allowed its intended function—and no more. It is the proper restoration of this law/gospel dynamic that, more than any other factor, will renew preaching and enrich its pastoral significance (see chap. 3).

Implicit in the preacher's task of relating texts to the gospel and of distinguishing promise from law, is theology's dialogue with the world of the listener. In all stages of sermon preparation and delivery the preacher is probing the mind and milieu of the listener. By analyzing the situation "out there" the minister is not indulging in culture criticism for its own sake, but is testing the appropriateness and the intelligibility of his or her gospel. There is only one gospel, but the core embodies many shapes. I also do not mean to imply that the preacher can ever set the relationship of culture and church into an easy law/gospel, them/us dialectic, as though one could preach to the cultured despiser in the world without addressing the cultured despiser who lives in oneself and in the "best" members of one's congregation. Theological analysis helps the preacher discover to what extent the "out there" dwells "in here," in preacher and congregation, and to what extent our culture colors our perception and expression of the gospel. Tillich's statement of the relationship between culture and gospel is by no means a simple question and answer. In fact, his formula is frustratingly circular:

> Symbolically speaking, God answers man's questions, and under the impact of God's answers man asks them. Theology formulates the question implied in human existence, and theology formulates the answers implied in divine self-manifestation under the guidance of the questions implied in human existence. [13]

For Tillich, theological analysis of culture serves a more integrative role than that of a *preparatio evangelii*. Yet his theology does not quite preach, for it lacks adequate distance from its audience. In this same vein Ernst Fuchs admonishes us: theology does not preach; it prepares for preaching. His warning, it seems to me, applies more to existential philosophy than to theology, but its concern is clear. We must establish a *theologically* sound conception of the listener's world before we can preach in it, to it, for it, or against it. [14]

The preacher-as-person lives in this world and ministers to it, but only the pastor-as-theologian can accurately assess the mobility, historicism, secularism, banal religiosity, and, most of all, the anxiety, of our age. And only the theological faculty of the preacher enables him or her to relate the human situation to the divine, enduring truths that cohere to the center, the eternal gospel. Beyond the preacher's pastoral experiences lies systematic theology's perennial dialogue with psychotherapy, anthropology, philosophy, ideology, politics, the arts, science, medicine, cybernetics, and ethics. This dialogue not only informs preaching; it makes it possible—and intelligible.

When one analyzes culture in theological terms, an old question of sermon-mechanics loses its urgency: where shall the preacher begin? With the contemporary, here-and-now? Or the biblical, then-and-there? When preaching begins with the contemporary situation, it views that situation through the lens of the eternal gospel. It is never data or commentary unrelated to the center. When preaching begins with the biblical situation, it never offers it as exegetical "background," as though, in Fosdick's famous quip, people really come to church with a burning interest in the Jebusites, but rather it always associates the biblical situation with contemporary needs. Thus the responsible preacher cannot outline the religious background of the Athenians (to cite an example in the book of Acts) without speaking of the current manifestations of humankind's abiding lust for religion. When the preacher projects all history and experience through the eternal prism, the infinite relevance of the gospel itself bridges the distance between the then-and-there and the here-and-now.

WHAT PREACHING DOES FOR THEOLOGY

To invert Ebeling's good sentence: Preaching is necessary in order to make theology as hard for the theologian as it has to be. Preaching turns theology back to its center, which is the gospel, and insists upon a gospel-based budgeting of theology's resources. Preaching requisitions Christ from theology. It demands formulations that necessitate the cross.

Preaching functions as a corrective of theology. When theology moves toward synthesis with its dialogue partners of other disciplines, preaching recalls for it its character as *theo*-logy, reflection on God. When theology becomes preoccupied with the symmetry of its own system, preaching reminds it of the catastrophic core of judgment and grace that called theology into being. When theology loses interest in the Scripture, preaching continues to wrestle with the Word—week-in, week-out. When theology becomes bogged down in words, the preached word continues to witness, in words, to an historical event. When theology looks with pessimism upon the vastness of the hermeneutical arch and the apparent impossibility of genuine understanding, preaching comforts it with a gospel that creates its own understandings and makes ready its own way. When theology produces unpreachable, that is, nonevangelical, words about God, preaching marks them REFUSED, and the church momentarily pauses, examines itself, and corrects its course.

Preaching is the first and final expression of theology. It is first in the sense that the Christian movement was born in preaching. Certainly, the first preaching we encounter, and indeed the *only* preaching we will ever encounter, is theological. What is the nature of this original theology of the New Testament? Preaching gives a clue. In preaching, theology recovers three elements it had at its origin: its kerygmatic impulse, its oral nature, and its character as worship.

The New Testament record has proved to be a proclamation, an anthology of preaching. The gospel "memoirs," as Justin Martyr called them, strangely omitted the very elements we find indispensable in biography. They contain nothing of Jesus' physical appearance, his early life, schooling, formative influences, and vocational decisions. The New Testament says little about his relationship with his parents, less about his siblings, and absolutely nothing about his attitude toward his own sexuality. Nor are we ever made privy to Jesus' thinking. We should have liked four "*zoe*graphies," records of his spiritual development. Instead, we are given an exteriorized "narrative of the things which have been accomplished" (Luke 1:1) whose organizing principle is the proclamation of salvation in Jesus Christ. The New Testament reads as a sermon whose *scopus*, to use a homiletic word, is the gospel. This is to say the primitive church filtered every datum about Jesus through the experience of resurrection, giving to its literary documents an arrow-like nisus toward death and new life (see chap. 2). Hence the foward-looking quality of the Gospel of Mark, for example, actually represents a reading *back* of all the Jesus stories in light of the transforming event of resurrection. This critical rediscovery, made by men who doubted the historical basis of much of the Gospels, has—ironically—provided a key for unlocking the meaning of the New Testament.

What is axiomatic to the Gospels applies also to the Epistles and to the primary source for our study of the primitive preaching, the book of Acts. Acts presents an outline of Christian preaching. Its distillation of the kerygma has been the subject of scholarly argument since the work of C. H. Dodd appeared in the 1930s. Without becoming embroiled in the debate, we can say that in the book of Acts, preaching incorporates assertions about the person, work, and future of Jesus, amounting to a theology of Jesus, all of which revolves around the core proclamation of his death and resurrection. Thus we do not ask the pointless question, Did preaching give rise to theology, or theology to preaching? for at their source, they were one. At its source, preaching was theological, and theology was proclamatory. To the pure historicity of the Jesus-event itself, before it was overlaid with theological proclamation or proclamatory theology, we can only offer the assent of adoration in which theology begins and ends.

Theology soon lost its kerygmatic character, as did preaching; and the church endured, indeed sponsored, seasons and seasons of aridity. Church reform invariably meant a return to the gospel, and as the late Archbishop Brilioth pointed out, every reform movement followed a vanguard of great preaching.[15] To the examples of the Waldenses, Franciscans, Dominicans, Lollards, Bohemian Brethren, Lutherans, Scottish Presbyterians, and Methodists, we might add the image of Martin Luther King and his associates marching in the streets, but also preaching from the pulpits of hundreds of churches throughout the South. In our era those theological movements that have sought to recapture the essence of the addressed promise of God, the gospel, have sprung from a concern for preaching—we need mention only the schools of Barth and Bultmann, represented in this chapter by Ott and Ebeling.

But how mischievous to offer preaching as a solution for unkerygmatic theology when preaching is such a well-documented part of the problem! When I suggest that preaching can do something *for* theology, by preaching I mean not the academic discipline, but preaching as the sum total of speakers, listeners, and settings throughout the church, that is, preaching as the ceaseless activity of the church. *That* preaching, by virtue of its name (*euangelizomai, kerusso, martureo*), its original commission, and its immediate accountability to the needs of the church, cannot stray as far from the gospel as can academic theology. Preaching's detours and experiments are too costly, and their results in the lives of people are too devastating to tolerate. Thus parish preaching, often unreflectingly and even unwillingly, serves as a guide and corrective for theology.

The second element of theology's original nature that it recovers in preaching is its orality (see chap. 4). The original proclamatory theology of the church was oral-aural. Our New Testament—both Epistles and Gospels—is a frozen record of oral discourse. Perhaps no one understood the oral nature of the Christian message better than Luther, who somewhere claims that "the Gospel should not be written but screamed" and promulgated a confessional definition of the gospel that totally bypassed its written character.[16] He held that "it is not at all in keeping with the New Testament to write books on Christian doctrine." Of the apostles he said, "Before they wrote, they first of all preached to the people by word of mouth and converted them, and this was their real apostolic and New Testament work." "However, the need to write books was a serious decline and a lack of the Spirit which necessity forced upon us; it is not the real manner of the New Testament."[17]

Surely, before preaching reminds theology of its oral possibilities, it needs to set its own house in order. So debased is preaching as an oral event that manuscripts are called sermons, and in some places seminarians are taught to preach by being made to read their manuscripts. And what we know of the gifted preachers, we too often discover via printed collections of the year's "best" sermons, usually selected according to non-oral, nonhomiletical criteria, such as the writer's academic respectability, poeticality of expression, or ecclesiastical reputation. As if the loss of authentic orality—by means of literary manuscript preaching, slide shows, liturgists in leotards, and similar events—were not bad enough, now many churches are distributing printed copies of the scriptural lessons for the day, so that when the lector says, "Hear the Word of God," the congregation in a single movement buries its nose in the bulletin. Much more could be said about the oral-aural nature of preaching. But our subject is the oral nature of theology.

I do not suggest that theology try to get along without its books, but I do wish for theology to recognize and appreciate its recessed oral-aural nature, which is evidenced in preaching and almost nowhere else. Debates and disputations, so long an anvil for hammering out theological positions, have all but disappeared from the scene, and in America even theology by conversation seems endangered. In Europe the traditional public defense of the doctoral thesis occasions only a gathering of appointed interlocutors, with perhaps a relative or two; while in America the "oral" either covers a limited and previously defined set of questions or confirms, as a formality, the examiners' attitude toward the written thesis. Among church judicatories, the postseminary interviews in which the candidate gives expression to his or her theological position had long been characterized by the rigor of a fraternity (or sorority) initiation—until the oversupply of clergy became significant. All of this is to say that, aside from the classroom (a huge exception, to be sure) theology has not valued and cultivated its oral nature.

The third contribution preaching makes to theology has to do with the context of worship in which theology originally arose. If the church's original theology was, in large measure, *heard* in events of proclamation, instruction, and worship, may not preaching help theology overcome its objectification into written formulas and books? Concerning the legalese of the Nicaean articles, for example, Frederick Crowe writes, "This is not the language of prayer. . . . Much less is it the joyful proclamation of the good news."[18] Once upon a time theology too was carried out in the spirit of worship. Theologians such as Augustine and Anselm, as well as many theologians of the Eastern tradition, offered their labors to God as sacrifices of adoration; Barth's postwar lectures at Bonn began at 7:00 A.M. with the singing of a psalm. In the ecclesiastical Latin of the fourth century, four hundred years before it was exclusively associated with preaching, *praedicare* meant "to praise," "to celebrate."[19] Perhaps preaching, which has retained its place in the context of worship, might communicate this dimension to systematic theology.

An intriguing first step has been taken by Geoffrey Wainwright, whose *Doxology: The Praise of God in Worship, Doctrine, and Life* is the only fullblown systematic theology constructed on the basis of the church's liturgical life.[20] We need to be alert to signals that theology is shifting on its foundation of doctrinal propositions and philosophical, psychological, political, and biological supports and is beginning to seek a footing in the church's own activity of worship. Unfortunately, of the 583 pages of text and notes dealing with the church's theology of worship, Wainwright devotes only two pages to preaching! Thus a potential theology of *praxis*, which is the fusion of words and deeds, is in this case deprived of its principle of interpretation. For the "five words" of the mind that Paul advocates in I Corinthians 14:19 are needed to provide balance and differentiation, even for the most liturgical forms of worship. Furthermore, preaching explains and presides over the necessary transition from liturgical praxis within the sanctuary to liturgical praxis understood as the reshaping of society. The word of preaching interprets liturgical action; it rescues liturgy in the sanctuary from formalism, and liturgy in the world from mere social activism. In the church, it tells why Christians "take and eat"; in the world, it tells why Christians must help others eat, find justice, and experience a fully human and dignified way of life. As the interpreter of both cultus and culture, preaching suggests new options for practical theology. With the flexibility of its movement from the church to the world, preaching makes the *doing* of theology less a slogan and more a real possibility for communities of Christians. It may even rehabilitate practical theology as *the* working theology of the church.

PREACHING AS THEOLOGY

Preaching is the final expression of theology. It has been toward preaching that theology has been tending. After the exegete has told us what the text once meant, and the systematician has told us what the text means in its historical, doctrinal, and philosophical setting, the preacher, to borrow Ebeling's phrase, executes the text by helping it to speak to a particular time, situation, and people. The majority of Christians encounters theology only in this, its final form, preaching.

If theology is, in Ott's words, "the reflective function of preaching itself," then preaching might be termed the *projective*, or public, function of theology itself. But how to make such an assertion without robbing the two disciplines of their unique character? E. L. Mascall has sternly warned against "the kind of philistinism which would reduce theology to homiletics and would repudiate any interest in scholarly questions as 'wisdom according to the flesh.' " He adds, "The relevance of a piece of research to the work of man's salvation may be remote and yet real."[21] While never accepting any stereotype of theology as an ivory-tower discipline, we might say that preaching engages the apparently remote, assimilates and internalizes it, and finally, not only makes it real, but integrates it in congregations of faith.

The movement from proclamatory theology to theological proclamation results in a three-fold confluence: in the preacher, in the Christian community, and in the sermon. In the preacher it means the end of "memo theology" carried on by means of occasional contacts between members of the several departments in the university or divisions within the theological faculty. The preacher *is* the exegete, systematician, domatician, historian, and pastor. The preacher becomes the embodiment of Schleiermacher's ideal theologian described in *Brief Outline of the Study of Theology*.

> When every individual, along with his own particular discipline, possesses also a general comprehension of the whole, is it possible for communication to take place between all and sundry; and thus is it possible for each, by means of the discipline to which he specially devotes himself, to exercise efficient influence upon the whole.[22]

The ministry of this ideal individual integrates all the theological disciplines into a *practical system* organized around the community's manifold experience of grace and publicly interpreted for the community by the proclaimed word. For those in ministry, this means that every aspect of preaching is theological; not only the restatement of scriptural words and themes, but the style with which they are restated; not only the words, but the posture and the sense of congruence between person and word; not only the message, but also the programs and congregational action by which the message is implemented. A boring sermon, an unimplemented sermon, an orthodox but discarnate sermon—are all theological statements.

Here we come to the confluence of disciplines in the sermon. Into the sermon pour exegesis, biblical theology, systematics, dogmatics, symbolics, apologetics, history, comparative religion, practical theology, liturgy, the wisdom of the nontheological disciplines, the experience and personality of the minister. Whenever the exegetical, systematic, or historical disciplines obtrude, the sermon is in danger of losing its unique character as an estuary, and the preacher must begin anew. For the sermon, as the projective function of theology, contains all, but only *in nuce*. It is a fragment, a nuance of the whole, yet contains the whole. Tillich writes, "A fragment is an implicit system; a system is an explicit fragment."[23] As fragments, sermons are no less rigorously designed than systems, but sermon structures differ according to the existential purpose of preaching and its fluid, fleeting mode of presentation. Systems tell the way things are; sermons tell what they might become. Not that sermons must be more kerygmatic than systems, but methods of measuring the kerygmatic impact of sermons differ radically from the canons by which systems are evaluated. Sermons are welded to interpersonal relationships and arise within the context of worship; systems abjure the personal or subjective and have largely lost their character as worship. For these and other reasons we still speak of the "mystery of preaching," but seldom of "the mystery of theology."

If the desired integration is to take place in theology, it may begin with the recognition of the legitimacy of preaching as a theological discipline. Preaching will be understood, not only as the last point on the theological continuum, but also as a moment of convergence in which all that we are about in theology is brought to expression.

II. *RESURREXIT:* POWER TO PREACH

The medieval priest robed in white greets the three townswomen before a makeshift tomb against the north wall of the chancel. On Good Friday the veiled crucifix from the high altar had been hidden in the tomb. But now it is Easter morning and something is afoot. "Whom do you seek in the tomb, O followers of Christ?" They reply, "Jesus of Nazareth, O visitor from heaven." With a flourish he opens the tomb to reveal only the veil while proclaiming for all in the church to hear: "He is not here; He is risen! Resurrexit Dominus!" Church bells begin to peal.

Christian preaching was born in the resurrection of Jesus. It happened in this way: one disciple, trembling, cried out in breaking, terrified voice, "Christ is risen!" And the receiver of the message made it a sermon by completing the circuit and exulting, "He is risen indeed!" Fifty-one Sundays of the year, only dimly do preachers remember this fountain of all preaching. It was resurrection that validated Jesus' ministry, his announcement of the Kingdom, his ethical teachings, and finally his death. No pagan reporter ever bothered to record the words or the substance of Christ's moral teachings, including the Sermon on the Mount, but in resurrection, and only in resurrection, everything—epileptic children, withered limbs, stilled storms, and all the wisdom and suffering that history usually sweeps under its carpet—became kerygmatically significant.[1] Let the reminder for preachers be: only because of the resurrection does Christian preaching assume the significance and importance so desperately claimed for it. I am speaking of resurrection, not as the annual subject of a sermon which somehow validates our unresurrected musings for the remainder of the year, but of resurrection as that which informs the character of preaching itself.

POWER TO PREACH

Kant's celebrated questions—What can I know? What ought I to do? What may I hope?—are answered in the theology of resurrection and, with varying degrees of success, in resurrection sermons. Although it is the final question, the question of hope, to which resurrection speaks most eloquently, it is not uncommon to hear Easter sermons that are preoccupied entirely with epistomological and historical issues and reasoned attempts to prove the factuality of the resurrection of Jesus and the reliability of the resurrection accounts. If the "What ought I to do?" question is raised at all, its answer usually bypasses the ethical, missiological, or liturgical imperatives of the Bible and comes home to roost on "gratitude."

This is not to underestimate the importance of the resurrection as an event. Although the deed of resurrection was immediately interpreted by words of proclamation, buttressed by appearances of all sorts, and embraced and developed by faith, the event retains priority. As even the most skeptical of commentators is likely to say, *something* happened. Historical analysis of eschatological events yields notoriously inconclusive results: there are testimonies already colored by faith, supernatural appearances and disappearances, and an explosion of "happenings" that defy chronological ordering. In short, the greater the obsession with historical proofs, the greater is the need of faith in the God who "has chosen things low and contemptible, mere nothings, to overthrow the existing order" (I Cor. 1:28 NEB). Nevertheless, just because the *something* that has happened is as resistant to historical analysis or laboratory testing as, say, the creation of the world or the call of Israel, it does not follow that the objectivity of the event, God's raising of Jesus in a particular time and place, must be given over to the realm of subjectivity. When Willi Marxsen interprets the resurrection as the miraculous and unexpected birth of faith,[2] certainly a grace-ful event whenever it occurs, he is simply fuzzing the point of the New Testament and the whole catholic tradition for which the grace of faith implies and demands the reality of an event outside itself. The witnesses say more than "I am certain"; they say, "It is certain."[3] Thus preaching walks the line between the *pro nobis* and *extra nos* accents of the resurrection, relinquishing neither. Contemporary faith scrutinizes the recorded, primitive faith of others, not as its final object of exploration, but as a window opening onto other realities. Despite the erudition with which Marxsen dismisses the resurrection as merely one of many possible metaphors for "the cause of Jesus," one cannot help but suspect that *his* reading of the faith has been colored and clouded by historical positivism. "Jesus is dead"[4] is an unflinchingly honest assessment of where his and all other subjective theories of resurrection leave the preacher. They bring with them an odor of death, which even the most kerygmatic-sounding paeans to the future cannot dispel.

The priority of the deed is essential to preaching, but it does not follow that the rhetorical form most appropriate to resurrection is historical apology, or even story, and most certainly not dogmatic explanations of the modes of Christ's presence. The resurrection is for proclamation. Jürgen Moltmann does away with the modern *need* to say more about the resurrection than the sources themselves say. He writes, "The Easter reports in the New Testament proclaim in the form of narrative, and narrate history in the form of proclamation. The modern alternative, reading them *either* as historical sources or as kerygmatic calls to decision, is foreign to them, as the modern distinction between factual truth and existential truth is also foreign to them."[5]

In the resurrection, God vindicated the crucified Jesus and made him Lord. "The God of our fathers raised Jesus whom you killed by hanging him on a tree. God exalted him at his right hand as Leader and Savior, to give repentance to Israel and forgiveness of sins" (Acts

5:30-31). The resurrection is about God. Feuerbach's interpretation of the doctrine of resurrection is representative of the perennial criticism, namely that resurrection merely symbolizes humankind's craven need for personal immortality and therefore serves only the greediest instincts of the human ego. Too many Easter sermons still reinforce this libel. But the belief in resurrection did not arise as an anthropological symbol of hope, but rather as a means of expressing faith in the righteousness of God. God's righteousness shall overcome. The doctrine's presenting problem was not the question of personal mortality, but rather, Why must the righteous suffer? Why must Israel be a reproach? The apocalyptist's answer—and the Christian preacher's answer—directs the questioner to consider, not only the past and the present, but the future as well.[6] Because God has raised Jesus, Jesus is no longer bound to the past; he has a future which he now shares with those who, like him, had been held captive by the past and the powers of sin, death, and Satan.

The history of theology and worship has been a history of the progressive separation of Good Friday and Easter. The righteousness of God demands their unity: the one who was rejected by the Jews and executed by the Gentiles was raised from the dead. His message and ministry, but most of all, the humiliating tool of his defeat, have been approved, vindicated, and glorified by God. God's righteousness is such that it can find its triumph only in the utter defeat of Jesus. By the same token, a Christian theology of the cross, no matter how poignant and realistic it is in its description of the Crucified One, cannot stop short of resurrection. Because of the resurrection of Jesus, theology is not limited to a chronological description of the world's stations of misery, just as Christians are never forced to experience cross without resurrection. For the resurrection now precedes and informs all theology, worship, Christian life—and preaching. When the book is slammed in the darkness of the Tenebrae service, resurrection is a surety whose presence cannot be imagined away even for the sake of Good Friday theatrics. When the medical verdict is "malignancy," there too, the resurrection hope forces its way into the consulting room to define this particular cross. The preaching of resurrection without crucifixion leads to questions like Risen from what? and gives rise to mindless "celebrations"—of what, no one is sure. The preaching of crucifixion without resurrection calls up questions like To what end? and produces predictable and manageable guilt trips for the congregation.

This righteousness of God does not rest upon an isolated death and the miraculous or magical resuscitation of a corpse. Jesus was no Lazarus; nothing of my hope is tied up in Lazarus. Lazarus is dead. The unified event of death and resurrection cannot be restricted to the past tense, which is the domain of Lazarus-like transitoriness. When Paul reminds Agrippa, "This was not done in a corner" (Acts 26:26), he conceivably might have been speaking of history as well as geography. For the resurrection of Jesus inaugurates the new age by proleptically revealing and enacting the drama of the age to come. He is "the first fruits of those who have fallen asleep" (I Cor. 15:20), the beginning of the end. For those in Christ, the concept of history has been both deepened and enlarged. For what happened to Christ is now in a real sense my history also, and the same Christ to whom I relate as a figure of the past, I now await as the bringer and consummator of the future. Moltmann makes the point, however, in distinction from Pannenberg, that we await, not merely the future and not even a future resurrection like Jesus', but we await the risen Christ in order to participate in *his* future.[7] Preaching belongs to this eschatological age; it never ceases to bear witness to it; it deepens and enlarges Christ's history for those who wait on him.

This is done most concretely in the preaching of the new creation. The risen Christ, as God's own promise of the cosmic restoration to come, establishes the genetic link between redemption and creation, between the soul's cultivation of heaven and humanity's care of the earth, between citizenship in the city above and participation in the city below. These concerns need not be understood as ethical addenda to the Christian faith or manifestations of Christian idealism. The only ideal Christianity knows is that which was historically realized in the person and work of Christ. His cross is the poignant and universal expression of human suffering, and his resurrection is the protest against it.[8] If you want to know where God stands on suffering and death, look at Good Friday—and Easter! As

William Sloane Coffin remarked in one of his Beecher lectures, those who love good but do not hate evil are doomed to sentimentality. Creation is no longer seen solely in light of the Fall, and Christ's resurrection signals more than a restoration of the groaning old creation. In Christ's resurrection, creation finds its true goal.

> He is the image of the invisible God, the first-born of all creation: for in him all things were created, in heaven and on earth, visible and invisible, whether thrones or dominions or principalities or authorities—all things were created through him and for him. He is before all things, and in him all things hold together (Col. 1:15-17).

From Paul, through Tertullian and the physicalism of the Greek fathers, to Teilhard de Chardin, the Christian tradition has managed to retain the cosmic proportions of resurrection without relinquishing the humanity of Jesus and the earthy, hylic quality of creation/new creation. Tertullian describes creation in this way in *On the Resurrection of the Flesh:*

> Recollect that God was wholly concerned with it and intent upon it, with hand, mind, work, counsel, wisdom, providence, and especially with that affection which prescribed its features. For whatever expression the clay took upon it, the thought was of Christ who was to become man.[9]

Likewise, it was Teilhard's latent theology of resurrection that called forth his mystical *Hymn to Matter:*

> You who batter us and then dress our wounds, you who resist us and yield to us, you who wreck and build, you who shackle and liberate, the sap of our souls, the hand of God, the flesh of Christ: it is you, matter, that I bless. I bless you, matter, and you I acclaim: not as the pontiffs of science or moralizing preachers depict you, debased, disfigured—a mass of brute forces and base appetites—but as you reveal yourself to me today, in your totality and your true nature.[10]

The earthy hope for new creation is expressed in most burial liturgies, which proclaim a bodily linkage, as it were, between, on the one hand, creation, the resurrection of Jesus, baptism, and the hope for the harvest of spiritual bodies, and on the other hand, the lifeless body, which is symbolic of the old creation. So the committal prescribed in the older Lutheran rite:

> May God the Father, who has created this body;
> May God the Son, who by his blood has redeemed this body together with the soul;
> May God the Holy Ghost, who by baptism has sanctified this body to be his temple—keep these remains unto the day of the resurrection of all flesh. Amen.

The promise of resurrection brings with it the commission and the power to preach. In fact, the resurrection of Jesus may not be distinguished from a call to witness and ministry. Just as Old Testament prophets were called through visions of the glory to come, the church received its marching orders in the risen Christ's preview of glory. This is emphasized in Matthew's Gospel, whose fused account of the resurrection and ascension of Jesus contains no fewer than three "go and tell" directives, which are skillfully contrasted with the chief priests' duplicitous "go and tell" issued to the soldiers. For Paul, the crucifixion and resurrection implied Israel's rejection of Jesus and opened the way for the Gentile mission. Paul's own vision of the risen Christ was his call to ministry and the prelude to a life of suffering. The call to preach did not lead inexorably to larger and larger churches, national recognition, financial security, and, finally, a prime-time show of his own. The call to preach had a rider attached: "For I will show him how much he must suffer for the sake of my name" (Acts 9:16). In II Corinthians 1:8-9, Paul reveals both the burden and the power of his ministry of preaching.

> For we do not want you to be ignorant, brethren, of the affliction we experienced in Asia; for we were so utterly, unbearably crushed that we despaired of life itself. Why, we felt that we had received the sentence of death; but that was to make us rely not on ourselves but on God who raises the dead.

FROM KERYGMA TO STORY

Paul's theology of the death and resurrection of Jesus made provision only for the fact *that* Jesus had been a man, had lived on earth, and had conducted an earthly ministry. These were but the raw materials for the decisive, salutary meaning associated with his death and resurrection.[11] Thus, as Leander Keck stated in a lecture on Romans, the Pauline "gospel" is not a narrative as much as it is a formula for Christ's entrance and exit from history. But historical figures generate stories, and historical people whose lives—and therefore whose consciousness—have a *plot* with a beginning, a middle, and an end, appropriate truth most effectively as story.[12] Augustine called preaching the *narratio* of God's love, a story that endures so long as God's plot from creation to Parousia continues.[13] When the Hebrew youngster seeks the meaning of the statutes and ordinances, the father is instructed to reply in narrative. "We were Pharoah's slaves in Egypt and . . ." (Deut. 6:20-25). Early Christianity circulated stories about Jesus, which the form critics labeled paradigms and Amos Wilder calls sub-plots, that effectively storified the kerygma in miniature.[14] An exorcism account, for example, says all there is to say about Christ's identity, authority, and power over the forces that separate mankind from God. Similarly, the parables of the kingdom, like the gospel of the resurrection itself, are all about *God* and *his* mysterious presence, *his* authority, *his* unexpected grace, and *his* future appearance.

Like the resurrection kerygma, stories also deepen and enlarge the hearer's sense of history. They deepen history by personalizing it; just when the hearer thinks a parable is an interesting little story about other kinds of people, he recognizes himself in the cast of characters. "Two men went up into the temple to pray . . ." Suddenly a story about two ancient characters is transformed into a disclosure of two religious people who *both* attend the temple, feel the need for prayer, and are in search of justification. The hearer is caught up in a situation in which she must immediately choose the character with whom she will identify and is forced to answer the questions, What *kind* of religious person shall I be? Where shall I find *my* justification? In his theses concerning the parables, Robert Funk aptly states, "Grace always wounds from behind, at the point where man thinks he is least vulnerable."[15]

Like the resurrection kerygma, the New Testament stories enlarge the hearer's history by opening it to the future. Indeed, Eugen Rosenstock–Huessy insists that *any* story must deepen the sense of commonality between teller and listener while it also leads both speaker and hearer into a new future.[16] This is deliberately done in the biblical story and its countless sub-plots. The main story awaits its thrilling conclusion, which, adds Jesus, only the author knows for sure (Mark 13:32). The parables, healings, and exorcisms end with directives, "Go and do likewise," "Go and sin no more," or their equivalent, taking the characters off stage and extending the grace of God into those future developments in their lives which the reader can only imagine—or enact for himself. The book of Acts is an unfinished narrative, and even the genuinely personal Epistles, despite their rounded-off conclusions, ought to be understood as episodes in the ongoing literary and pastoral relationship which Paul plans to sustain with his congregations. So the eschatological resurrection of Jesus has its echoes in the openendedness of the Christian story(ies). Preachers who would be storytellers must remember, then, the chief function of the story is not to nail down a point, but to invite participation in the continuing story; not to illustrate the way things are, but to tell what they might become.

Preaching has invested heavily in the recent emphasis on narrative, sometimes without examining its own motives and the hermeneutical limits of storytelling. By narrative, most homiletical literature has meant the close embrace of *my* story and *the* story as a unified vehicle of good news. Not only is the ease of the movement from *the* story to *my* story often overestimated, but the many ways in which a story as an aesthetic object can actually widen the distance are usually overlooked. In some stories there are characters, emotions, and twists of plot with which I *cannot* identify. It is possible that a parable's allegorical framework, underdeveloped characterization, abbreviated storyline, ambiguous message, or obscure "point"—now lost in the recesses of early conflict between

Jewish and Gentile Christians—could obstruct, rather than enhance, my experience of God's grace. Every work of art selects an audience, including some, excluding others. For example, the parable of the Pharisee and the Tax-collector, which we considered above, works well when addressed to a religious audience; in fact, it requires a religious audience. But the same parable might not communicate as effectively to an audience for which church attendance, prayer, pious self-discipline, and the conscious quest for justification are not serious issues. Moreover, the members of this secularized audience cannot be written off as those who "wouldn't be caught dead in church," for they are in our churches—and in our pulpits—every Sunday morning. This is the risk of making stories; aesthetic objects come with built-in limitations.

A second danger lies in the story's telling. That story is an essential means of communicating the gospel, no one can doubt, but one searches in vain for the hermeneutical control that will deliver congregations from impressionistic exegesis (Raymond Brown's term for "How I felt when I read this text"), homemade parables, public recitals of the preacher's struggles, breakthroughs, passages, etc., etc., and all the ways in which the "Me Decade" has conscripted *the* story into the service of *my* story. I cannot imagine a clearer illustration of this than storyteller Sam Keen's advice: "For the moment, at least, we must put all orthodox stories in brackets and suspend whatever remains of our belief-ful attitude. Our starting point must be individual biography and history. If I am to discover the holy, it must be in *my* biography and not in the history of Israel."[17] The old warning against pulpit stories in which the preacher is the hero still holds true. Beware of sermons that begin, "When I was privileged to serve . . . " and end, "Therefore, being in touch with myself, I am. . . . " In the delicate balancing of the gospel and the preacher's experience of it (which *is* an indispensable dimension of preaching), we must recognize our bottomless capacity for self-deception in the many subtle ways we subordinate God's story to our own.

At the center of the Christian story that God gave his people is the passion narrative culminating in the event of Christ's resurrection.

Yet the resurrection itself, apart from stories of the empty tomb, the post-resurrection appearances of Jesus, and the church's experience of itself as resurrected, could not be presented in story form. Early and modern attempts to storify the event itself, such as the apocryphal Gospel of Peter's gargantuan Jesus who bursts forth with cross in hand, or Pär Lagerkvist's *Barabbas*, whose hero "watches" the resurrection, have ended in theological and often aesthetic failure. (Faulkner termed A *Fable*, his attempt at a fictional portrayal of Christ's death and resurrection, "my greatest failure.")

The resurrection event itself is not reported but proclaimed. It is, in fact, pure proclamation. *Resurrexit!* It tells not only the way things happened, but the way things are—with God, the cosmos, human destiny—and me. The Epistles preceded the written Gospels, and the church continues to hold the stories of Jesus in balance with Paul's more direct proclamation and application of the kerygma. To sermons the Gospels give the plot, and the Epistles give the theological structure, neither of which may be dismissed from the pulpit. Paul translated his experience of the risen Christ into a proclamation that he repeatedly told as *his* story, but also attempted to "prove" from history, and finally offered as an argument from which he was unafraid to draw conclusions and deduce implications (I Cor. 15:20 ff.; I Thess. 4:13-14). The proclamation of Christ's death and resurrection is always followed by an authoritative, direct, and existential "Therefore" (as in Romans 5:1), which connects the salvation-event with the stories of our lives.

THE KERYGMATIC PLACE

In a surburban Protestant congregation, worshipers at Easter dawn enter an unlighted, undecorated sanctuary with altar stripped and organ silenced. After public confession, the exchange of spoken versicles and responses concludes with a question and an invitation: "Why do you seek the living among the dead?" and "Come, see the place where He lay." The congregation quietly processes into a nearby woods to a rough-hewn cross. There, after lessons, hymns, and choral anthems, the preacher mounts a soapbox-like pulpit and with no uncertain sound becomes a herald of victory. Following the proclamation, the congregation, this time singing, trudges through the spring mud and enters a church marvelously transformed with light, lilies, azaleas, music, and paraments white and gold. The worshipers immediately celebrate the *therefore* connecting the event of Christ's resurrection and the stories of their lives by joining the risen Christ in a breakfast of bread and wine. This kind of exercise of historical imagination, paralleling the religious drama described in the epigraph to this chapter, is repeated throughout churches of all traditions in all places. At the center of the pageantry, however, and keeping an austere distance from subjective feelings and experiences, is *God's* answer to every questionable or interrupted human story: *Resurrexit!*

Where may we find the place at which discussion gives way to proclamation, analysis to adoration, and assent to participation? In short, what is resurrection's most appropriate environment? It is the worshiping community. Death and resurrection—this fugal theme is at the center of Christian worship. The drama of the church year unfolds it; the Sunday service, which originated as a little Easter, reenacts it. Baptism as burial and resurrection in Christ, sacramentally recapitulates it, and the Holy Communion represents it. [18] The first and only feast of the church was the Pasch, the two-day vigil that commemorated the death and resurrection of Jesus in a single, fused experience, beginning with baptisms on Holy Saturday and culminating in the Eucharist at Easter dawn. This unitive feast, along with the priority of Sunday as the Lord's Day, provide an early clue to how the mind of the church will work: it will orchestrate its preaching, spiritual discipline, and liturgical and sacramental life according to the rhythm of death and resurrection.

When Jesus came out of the tomb, the people of God came out with him. Paul says that God has "made us alive together with Christ . . . and raised us up with him, and made us sit with him in the heavenly places" (Eph. 2:5-6). In a variety of sacramental and liturgical ways the church affirms the corporate character of the resurrection of Jesus. The pagan Celsus complained that everybody saw Jesus die, but only a crazed woman and a few fanatics saw him alive again. Every Easter someone in the adult discussion class asks why the risen Christ didn't appear to Herod or Caiaphas or Pilate, as though such an appearance would have cleared up a lot of misunderstandings. Peter's speech in Acts 10 alludes to the question. "But God raised him on the third day and made him manifest; not to all the people but to us who were chosen by God as witnesses, who ate and drank with him after he rose from the dead" (vv. 40-41). The newness of life that the church now enjoys through its Lord is a continuation of the historical experience of eating and drinking with Jesus. As the narrative of Jesus' appearance to Thomas indicates, the question of *how* one meets the risen Christ was a vexing one for the church. The Emmaus Road incident, in which Jesus is known in the breaking of the bread, provides an answer: we meet him and experience his resurrection as we always have—in community with one another, in the opening of the Scripture, and in the sacramental breaking of bread. Only in this context can discourse about the resurrection become resurrection preaching.

We have seen that the gospel of the resurrection and its many paradigmatic stories serve to deepen and enlarge the listener's sense of history. They invite personal participation, and they open onto a future consummation in the risen, returning Christ. All these strands, including the corporate nature of resurrection, are gathered together in the rich and textured fabric of worship. Here the worshiper experiences the interplay of story and proclamation, and discovers another way, the original way, in which human beings come to participate in the life story of God: we are baptized into the death and resurrection of Jesus (Rom. 6:3-5). Likewise, in the Eucharist the personal words of assurance—"given and shed for you"—are balanced by corporate thanksgiving, prayer, and adoration, and a sense of the congregation's responsibility to be in mission. Like all God's stories, the worship service is open-ended, and the congregation departs with some version of the old dismissal ringing in its ears: *Ite, missa est.* Not "Go, you are released," but "Go, you are sent." Like preaching, worship combines elements of story with pure proclamation. What else is the liturgy but the recital of God's story—from the song of the angels in the *Gloria in excelsis* to the awesome chant of the cherubim and seraphim in the *Sanctus*—interspersed with kerygmatic interpretation? All this is to say, too briefly, that preaching lives, moves, and has its being in this environment. When it disregards its liturgical matrix, preaching becomes the individualistic, virtuoso performance with which many Protestants are familiar, and thereby diminishes both itself and the church.

RESURRECTION PREACHING

Preaching, to be *preaching*, reenacts and participates in the defeat and victory of Jesus. As Eduard Schweizer remarked in a lecture, the resurrection of Jesus was an event of communication in which the whole personal being of Jesus radiated wholeness to others. Similarly, in its own moment of communication, preaching exposes the difference between death and hope in the lives of those who are participating in the sermon. This preaching separates our stories from God's story, reveals their radical differences, and with the proclamation of the gospel, sutures them again. This separating and binding of stories is the work of God.

If Christian preaching—in its content and its craft—is to have the character of death and resurrection, something in it must die. The same Paul who said, "I have been crucified with Christ; it is no longer I who live, but Christ who lives in me" (Gal. 2:20), also wrote, "For we preach not ourselves, but Christ Jesus the Lord; and ourselves your servants for Jesus' sake" (II Cor. 4:5 KJV). In terms of the message, what dies is the self-preoccupation that has gradually changed the herald into a gatekeeper through whose psyche every word of the Lord must pass. As servants of the Word we will dare to become generalists in an age of ego specialization. In terms of oral delivery or style, what dies is the old exhibitionism that elevates the sermon above the rest of the liturgy and the sacraments. May the preacher say of his or her craft what a church-arts designer said of his: "I don't want my work to call attention to itself. After the service one worshiper may say to another, 'Did you notice the candelabrum?' The other will reply, 'No, but come to think of it, it *was* beautiful.' "

Resurrection preaching has these implications: it takes death seriously, denying neither death nor the alienation, loneliness, anxiety, sin, and evil which cluster around it. Realism about death takes its cue from the Bible. In no gnostic resurrection myth nor in the assurances of positive/possibility thinking is the following dialogue likely to occur: *Jesus:* "Take away the stone." *Martha:* "Lord, by this time he stinketh" (John 11:39 KJV).

In I Corinthians 15 Paul is using what appears to be a homiletical device by holding up to his congregation the ghastly consequences of life and death without resurrection: " . . . If Christ has not been raised from death, then we have nothing to preach and you have nothing to believe" (15:14 TEV). He does not mean that there would be nothing to say; of course there would be plenty to say about immortality, Spring, renewal, heightened consciousness—but nothing to preach. Nothing to preach?

In that compartment of the collective unconscious reserved for preachers, a dream, a kind of nightmare, circulates freely. In it, the minister has been appointed to preach before a huge, expectant congregation. But an impediment arises: the preacher is caught in a traffic jam outside the church, or his notes disappear, or for agonizingly long minutes he searches the Bible in vain for his text. The people grow unruly and begin to file out of the church. In a state of complete disorganization and confusion, the preacher decides to make an attempt at his sermon, but discovers to his horror that he has nothing to say. Does this dream, shared by many preachers, simply reflect a fear of public speaking, a need for public approval, or does it testify to a deeper theological ambivalence? Nothing to preach!

Perhaps you have heard the evangelism pitch that asks, "How would you like to live in a community with no churches?" The question is supposed to conjure in the "prospect's" mind a picture of a community bereft of divine influences: no one to open Rotary with prayer; no benediction upon football squads as they prepare for mutual mayhem; no divine sanctions with which to decorate community values. But Paul's image of the absence of a risen God cuts deeper than that of a moribund Christendom. His manner of speech is neither a homiletical device nor a worked-out philosophical dialectic. For Paul can remember a time when cross and resurrection did not always form an inseparable unity, a time when the finality of Good Friday was a non-negotiable item in his religious package. He has experienced the nothingness of death without resurrection and desperately wishes to convey that futility: "We deserve more pity than anyone else in all the world" (I Cor. 15:19 TEV). Correspondent Ernie Pyle reported the mood at a briefing of World War II bomber pilots, soon to embark upon an impossible mission. The prevailing emotion, he said, was not fear, but a profound reluctance to give up the future.

A second implication of the resurrection is that preaching bears in its own fiber a note of victory. We have maintained as a real possibility and an accurate memory a vision of humankind "having no hope and without God in the world" (Eph. 2:12) in order not to minimize the catastrophic impact of God's victory over death. We do not preach about the resurrection week after week, but we do resurrection preaching by which the life of the risen Christ is made accessible to those who are dying in sin and despair. This was the preaching method of John Wesley, who, in the place of a single sermon on the resurrection, brought resurrection to bear upon the meaning of existence under a wide variety of biblical and theological themes.[19] The *how* of this appropriation of resurrected life belongs to the chemistry of Word and Spirit and will be explored in the following chapter. From the human vantage, the listener reenacts the preached word's reenactment of the movement from defeat to victory, "and then the passion of Christ and his resurrection come into force."[20] The note of victory implied in the original, technical meaning of our word "gospel" may not take the form of up-beat stories, victorious-living motifs, or the satisfied style of an oratory full of itself. But resurrection preaching will have an intensity and a joy about it derived from the divine drama and the whole congregation's experience of it. And in that moment of communication the gathered people of God will find the resources for endurance in the present day and hope for a future they are unwilling to relinquish.

III. HOW LAW AND GOSPEL WORK IN PREACHING

That I may rise, and stand, o'erthrow me, and bend
Your force, to break, blow, burn and make me new.

John Donne
Holy Sonnet[14]

Once there was a man who desperately needed to hear the word of God. He was an alcoholic trying to dry out and begin the life-long journey toward recovery and wholeness. His wife and children had gone, and, now that he had quit drinking, the job in which he had mindlessly subsisted had become hateful and oppressive to him. His loneliness was the kind that lives in boardinghouses, public libraries, all-night cafes, and even in churches. And his fear was the truest and purest of anxieties, that of a dark and unknown future. One night after an A.A. meeting, he wandered into a nearby church's Lenten worship and there for the first time in his life heard the gospel in all its comfort and power. What follows is a description of how that word fell upon his ears and heart. We should not attach too much significance to one case study; we could as easily consider the story of a confused teenager, a husband and wife struggling with marital difficulties, a successful but bored shopkeeper, a resident of the local nursing home, or a worn-out executive about to be discarded by his firm. What is offered here is not a Christian soap opera nor a prescriptive formula for successful preaching, but a kind of phenomenology of law and gospel as that dynamic *works* in all Christian preaching.

The man heard a sermon on Ephesians 2:1-10.

And you he made alive, when you were dead through the trespasses and sins in which you once walked, following the course of this world, following the prince of the power of the air, the spirit that is now at work in the sons of disobedience. Among these we all once lived in the passions of our flesh, following the desires of body and mind, and so we were by nature children of wrath, like the rest of mankind. But God, who is rich in mercy, out of the great love with which he loved us, even when we were dead through our trespasses, made us alive together with Christ (by grace you have been saved), and raised us up with him, and made us sit with him in the heavenly places in Christ Jesus, that in the coming ages he might show the immeasurable riches of his grace in kindness toward us in Christ Jesus. For by grace you have been saved through faith; and this is not your own doing, it is the gift of God—not because of works, lest any man should boast. For we are his workmanship, created in Christ Jesus for good works, which God prepared beforehand, that we should walk in them.

How did the man hear the sermon? He did not merely organize it into logical divisions, although for the sake of understanding he did do that. He did not merely sift it for a theme, although for the sake of coherence he unconsciously did that also. Least of all did he consciously grade the preacher's integration of textual study, theology, humanistic wisdom, liturgics, and communications skills. Although the preacher was blessed with warmth, dynamism, and style, the man never saw or heard any of these as elements separable from the sermon.

In a totally unanalytic way he made the message his own by accepting it as good news *pro me*. Instead of hearing the sermon as an alien word, he greeted it and welcomed it home. In this process of internalizing the word he replicated, or "printed," not just the sounds and meanings of individual words, but the dynamic of the message itself. He *moved*—with the exposition of the text, with the author, with Christ, with the preacher, and with his fellow worshipers—from death to life.

ANALYSIS, TRANSITION, INTEGRATION

In the sermon on Ephesians 2, the lonely man, the man without family and community, heard an analysis of what it means to be dead in sin and by nature a child of wrath. The analysis reached him as a word of judgment—for two reasons. First, in its accuracy it mirrored for him the futility of his own life. When the preacher spoke of sin, not as a series of individual actions, but as the penalty for a greater blindness in which we all once walked, he was at that point drilling without novocain. When the preacher explained wrath, not as God's petulant anger, but as a near-ontological misery in humankind, his listener was visited with the pain of self-recognition as he had never before experienced it. "So this is who I am!" he thought.

Second, the analysis came to him as the judgment of *God*. The preacher was not reflecting psychological theories, but was announcing a rift so deep and pervasive that it can only be *believed*. "The wrath of God," said Paul, "is *revealed* from heaven" (Rom. 1:18, emphasis added). Meaninglessness, guilt, anxiety, finitude—Tillich has identified these and other "laws" of life as the structures of existence. They remain neutral and unexplained categories, however, until they are set in the context of humanity's estrangement from God.[1]

When the man heard the law, it served as a reflector of his life and as an announcement of God's displeasure. It raised his consciousness and hammered his conscience. It both exposed and accused.[2] In its exposition of the man's alienation, the sermon—as law—drew upon the classical view of sin as privation, that is, the absence of completion that prohibits a being from fulfilling its own nature. In its indictment of human rebellion, it gave expression to the Reformation tendency to bring all sin under the aegis of concupiscence, which, in Luther's words, is "a nausea toward the good, a loathing of light and wisdom and a delight in error and darkness."[3] What is sinful is, not our finitude, but our perverse refusal to recognize it. It is not humanity's immature development, but its utter contempt for the Creator, which has provoked the wrath of God. So profound and inexplicable is this contempt that in Romans 1 it moves Paul to a doxological interlude.

At the epicenter of the Ephesians text, the writer introduces a transitional phrase so powerful that it interrupts his own exposition of wrath: "But God. . . . " God interrupts his own wrath with his own love. Suddenly the man was brought into the center of the gospel, because the God from whom he was so hopelessly estranged had drawn nigh in the message of Jesus. In Christ, God reestablishes his own identity as a giver of gifts and surprises. The lonely man was told that his destiny had been linked with Christ's, that new life in the risen Lord meant a new kind of life on earth and the promise of greater fulfillment "in the coming ages." As the preacher unfolded the text for the congregation, his sermon was heard with varying degrees of intensity—but one man, at least, heard it as an offer from God which brought with it the power to change his life. It was not an offer of something God might do, nor was it an exhortation to "get saved," but it was indicative perfect: "By grace you have been saved." God has already done it. Not only that, he has done it for you.

Finally, the man heard and began to experience the possibility of integration that belongs to those who have exchanged death for life. Vaguely he understood that this wholeness was in some way a *re*-integration of a life that was not originally meant to be fragmented. That God had designed him for the purpose of doing good works in Christ Jesus was both comforting and challenging. As a boy he had never heard the Christian life promoted in any terms other than, "*If* you want to get right with the Almighty, *then* this is what you *ought* to do." But that night the preacher had his grammar straight: "*Because* of God's grace . . . this *therefore* is what you *can* do. Become what you are!"

The three movements of the sermon—analysis, transition, integration—have their counterparts in the vocabularies of many theologians and teachers of preaching.[4] The terms are not as important as the realities they represent. Also, it is essential that the reader understand that what we are considering here are *not* design motifs, as though we were advocating a return to the predictable three-points-and-a-poem of yesteryear, but rather those *theological* movements which continue to appear in sermons of every shape and design.

THE DIVINE DIALECTIC

The preaching of the gospel—whether from the Old or New Testament—is always dialectical. Dialectic implies two interacting forces within the unitive Word of the one God, addressed to whole persons. But the dialectic is not limited to words. Israel lived out these two ways of hearing God's Word. Our preaching participates in the dialectic of salvation history, which begins with primal unity in God (call it original righteousness, *Imago dei*, or the truly human) and, depending on the scriptural source, moves from this original unity through one or more of the following sets of antitheses:

chaos to order	debt to forgiveness
bondage to deliverance	separation to reconciliation
rebellion to obedience	wrath to love
accusation to vindication	judgment to righteousness
despair to hope	defeat to victory
guilt to justification	death to life

1. The Long and Twisted Story

The first word in each pairing is reported as "bad news" for humanity and comes under the shorthand theological expression: law. Here we make no thorough attempt to sort through the several notions of law in the Old and New Testaments. The law is a body of divine regulations and a condition of existence (wrath, enmity with God) which characterizes those who have failed to keep God's commands. We do not perpetuate the simplistic pattern in which Old Testament = law and New Testament = gospel. Each testament contains commandments and admonitions that bring with them either threats or reports of divine punishment of those who have failed to carry them out. The "Thou shalt not" of Sinai has echoes, if not exact correspondences, in the warnings of Jesus in the Sermon on the Mount, the catalogues of vices (e.g., I Cor. 6:9), and the exhortations "in the Lord" of the Pauline Epistles (e.g., I Thess. 4:1-8), and in the aphoristic injunctions of the book of James. Likewise, in both testaments God's comforting promise can be heard and his mighty acts of salvation witnessed. Our concern is only to hear the two tones of God's word in relation to one another—both in Scripture and in history.

The grace of God underlies the giving of the law in the Old Testament, where it is not received as bad news by the people of God. In both testaments the law is the holy revelation of God's will for his people, embodying his perfect guidance and instruction. The psalmist can say, "Oh, how I love thy law!" (Psalm 119:97a); and Jesus assures the fledgling Christian community, "not an iota, not a dot, will pass from the law until all is accomplished" (Matt. 5:18b). Indeed, in many places *law* assumes the qualities and functions we associate with the word *gospel*. This partially explains the confusion and controversy generated by Barth's definition of the law: "The Law is nothing else than the necessary *form of the Gospel*, whose content is grace."[5]

The long and twisted story of Israel records the history of conflict between the two tones of God's word. It is a history of warnings and promises, violations and restorations, of bondage and deliverance, exile and homecoming, of Israel's harlotry and God's faithfulness. In almost predictable fashion, Israel's greatest prophets knock the people down with mighty judgments only to pick them up with words of consolation like those of Jeremiah: "And it shall come to pass that as I have watched over them to pluck up and break down, to overthrow, destroy, and bring evil, so I will watch over them to build and to plant, says the Lord" (31:28).

In one of his sermons Paul Scherer reminds us that the apostle Paul was converted to Christ from religion, not irreligion. This fundamental truth colored Paul's view of the law, which, since postexilic days, had stood in supreme independence from its moorings in the covenant and the worship life of the people. As a religious object it had taken on a power of its own, which, in Paul's view, not only condemns sin and works wrath, but also engenders its own system of gaining merit before God—apart from Christ and his cross. This law was given like mass vaccinations during an epidemic for the purpose of controlling a virulent outbreak of sin. What it controls, the gospel heals. That the law does not represent God's definitive means of dealing with human existence can be substantiated by Paul's insistent reminder to the Galatians (chap. 3) that the covenant of promise preceded the law by 430 years, or by Jesus' simple refutation of the laws controlling divorce: "From the beginning it was not so" (Matt. 19:8b). Certainly this "ministry of death," as Paul names the law in II Corinthians 3:7, is an "official" expression of God's purpose, just as the coroner's signed certificate is official. "For if a law had been given which could make alive, then righteousness would indeed be by the law" (Gal. 3:21b).

2. *The Death and Resurrection of the Mediator*

Despair lives on the edge of grace. One who hears the judgment of God is not far from the kingdom of God. The Old Testament's antiphon to judgment is the gospel of:

the covenant	the messianic promise
the new covenant	return from exile
deliverance from Egypt	the reign of God
God's love for the lowly	the Day of the Lord

In continuity with the Old Testament gospel, Jesus announced his messianic program in the "Nazareth Manifesto."

The Spirit of the Lord is upon me,
because he has anointed me to
    preach good news to the poor.
He has sent me to proclaim release
    to the captives
and recovering of sight to the blind,
to set at liberty those who are oppressed,
to proclaim the acceptable year of the Lord. (Luke 4:18-19)

The New Testament gospel addresses the realities of defeat, blindness, oppression, and every other situation in which the presence of a gracious God is desperately needed. Preaching carries on the work of God's incarnation; it remembers that God did not merely become a person, but a poor person, and that he identified with human pain in order to defeat it. Whenever preaching is separated from pastoral participation in suffering, its proclamation of God's victory sounds a hollow and discarnate note.

We anchor our preaching in the story of Jesus, which recapitulates the history of Israel and the destiny of all people. He enjoyed primal unity with God, experienced the shattering of it in the sin of the world, and was recreated by God to greater glory. Those joined to him through faith and baptism follow the same cycle to the same destination. But it is not easy. In words suggestive of the epigraph to this chapter, the young Luther wrote, "Whom God wants to heal, He first batters to pieces." The cycle of healing does not imply simple development, as though one might evolve from a condition of judgment into a state of forgiveness, but rather expresses the dialectical conflict between God and the forces of evil. God battles chaos for the purpose of creating order from it, and the people of God continue to live out that divine war against the forces of disintegration. Because Jesus defeated the last enemy, death, the Christian hope resides, not in the developmentalism of immortality, but in the radical transformation of resurrection. Christian preaching follows the dialectic in its offer of human wholeness, in which the identity of the old, sinful, defeated person is put to death, and yet preserved and taken up into a new reality of life, forgiveness, and victory. Eberhard Jüngel describes God as a "unity of life and death to the advantage of life."[6] The new life represents a restoration "with interest," as St. Thomas said, of an original and constitutive harmony with God. God's creatures now lay claim to the fullness of their humanity only insofar as they are "in Christ" and aware of the dialectics of Christian existence. "I have been crucified with Christ; it is no longer I who live, but Christ who lives in me" (Gal. 2:20a).

3. The Real World

Our student newspaper runs a little column of national news called "The Real World" in order to remind us of the larger realities outside basketball, sororities, and university politics. What can we say of this divine dialectic whose movements we have traced in the history of God's people and in the life of God's Son? Is this another neat theological construct at work everywhere except in the real world, applicable to everyone but real people? Will it produce, as Sir Karl Popper said of Hegel's dialectical method, real rabbits out of metaphysical silk hats? Does the death and resurrection of Jesus become, as it did in Hegel's system, a mere illustration of a grander and more abstract truth? Is judgment and grace a simple stencil we can lay over any biblical text to achieve the desired results?

Perhaps we ought to return to the alcoholic who desperately needed to hear the word of God. As I see him sitting out there in the near-darkened church, I do not recollect a category of alienation, *Angst*, malaise, or existential despair. He was *not* "modern man"! He *was* a lonely, anxious, despairing person. To this real person, the preacher conveyed not just a word of peace, mercy, or righteousness, but the living Christ, whose goodness at that moment was peace-shaped. By linking the story of Christ and the stories of those who listened, the preacher broke open precious theological treasures in order to disclose the presence of the living Christ in them. With "wrath" and "mercy" laid open, the incense of Christ himself filled the church. Like all sermons, this one participated in the continuing struggle between the nominal and the real, and that night, for a change, realism won. Finally, the event was real in that it was transacted between one living person and another. The man in the congregation did not read the sermon nor construct it from the pointillism of electronic impulses which is Jerry Falwell or Oral Roberts, but he experienced it "live" in the context of corporate worship, pastoral care, and the possibility of new relationships in Christ.

Whenever we are tempted to dismiss the judgment-grace dialectic as an exercise in nominalism, let us remember that even in our redeemed state we are all born (again?) legalists to whom grace remains an unnatural and often surprising intrusion. The law of this aeon continues to menace our marriages, our relationships with our parents and children, our contributions to society, and our life in the church. In these and other sectors of life, the difference between law and gospel, far from being a theoretical distinction, can mean the difference between existence under constant obligation and existence in the freedom of God. That this is true of *Christians* in community was documented by the most massive sociological study of any denomination in the United States. The authors discovered that none of the controversial issues in the church can be dealt with apart from an understanding of the basic polarity between law-oriented and gospel-oriented people. "Here is the fundamental reality of life within the church. Every move, every program, every rhythm of church life is affected by this polarity. No response to an issue, problem or program is complete unless it is set against this polarity first and framed in the light of this reality."[7]

Before the judgment-grace polarity among Christians was documented by sociologists it was asserted by a theologian. In Romans 7, Paul offers himself as a case study in the conflict:

> So I find it to be a law that when I want to do right, evil lies close at hand. For I delight in the law of God, in my inmost self, but I see in my members another law at war with the law of my mind and making me captive to the law of sin which dwells in my members. Wretched man that I am! Who will deliver me from this body of death? (vv. 21-24)

Many interpreters find it impossible to believe that the "I" of Romans 7 is Paul the Christian. Is it possible such weakness and corruption could exist in the man who has just written, "How can we who died to sin still live in it?" (6:2). If Paul is only describing the non-Christian or pre-Christian condition through converted eyes, which is today the accepted interpretation of this passage,[8] our preaching of the law has been rendered a harmless exercise in memory. In that case, the law serves *Christians* only as a friendly guide to good works and in no other capacity. Its work of mirroring evil and judging sin is reserved for those outside the Christian faith. It no longer applies to Christians, in whom the conflict between judgment and grace has ceased to rage.

But do we really know any such Christians? Do we know any who are exempt from the struggle between flesh and Spirit (Gal. 5) or who are beyond the range of Luther's call to daily baptismal renewal? In the real world, we never preach to people who are perfectly whole or hopelessly corrupt but only to those who are being healed or getting sick. We preach the reflecting/accusing law to those yet-contested territories in the Christian life, and with an eye to that outlying region of which Paul confessed, "Not that I have already obtained this or am already perfect; but I press on to make it my own, because Christ Jesus has made me his own" (Phil. 3:12).

There are, aside from the dictates of experience, compelling reasons for accepting at face value the ambiguity reported in Romans 7 as part and parcel not only of Paul's life, but of every Christian life.[9] Nothing in the context or flow of Paul's thought indicates to us that he is stepping outside himself to characterize life without Christ or his own preconversion existence. Indeed, the context indicates the reverse. Romans 7 is written in the present tense. Paul's analysis of this "I" torn between good and evil does *not* adequately describe the hedonism of life without God, which he has criticized elsewhere, nor does it do justice to the placid self-satisfaction of his own life under the law. It does capture both the wretchedness of Christians suspended between the aeons, *and* the deliverance that surpasses humanity's best efforts to save itself. We are delivered *by* conflict, not *from* conflict.

Christians now experience the law through their relationship with the gospel. The two tones are sounded together. It is like listening to a bassoon and a flute playing the same note. If I ask, Where does God's law strike home to me, the answer is not the Decalogue or isolated moral principles. I hear the law as I cooperate in "the sin of the world," which is the denial of Christ. I hear the law whenever I realize that in some way I have become an enemy of the cross of Christ (Phil. 3:18). The imperatives that, mysteriously, both accuse *and* encourage me now derive from my Christian faith: "Only let your manner of life be worthy of the gospel of Christ" (Phil. 1:27) or "If any man would come after me, let him deny himself and take up his cross and follow me" (Matt. 16:24).

The fluidity of law and gospel points more to a method of listening than a doctrine. Thus the death of Jesus reveals God's wrath *and* love; the call to discipleship both stings and encourages the Christian; the parable of the Pharisee and the Publican sends a decidedly mixed message, depending on the character with whom we identify. The fluidity of terms and life-situations takes the urgency out of the protracted controversy between Barthians and Lutherans over gospel and law. [10] If the unbeliever hears the content of the gospel first, that gospel will inevitably convey a sense of distance and alienation from God—which is law-talk—before the good news actually does its liberating work. No matter what their order of presentation, gospel and law (or *vice versa*) still sound the two tones of God's holy word.

The distinction between law and gospel takes place in the church, which is the body of forgiven sinners. The Holy Spirit cares for the church and only there creates the conditions in which law and gospel may be rightly heard. The work of distinguishing between law and gospel is best handled by parish preachers endeavoring to minister and communicate in the real world. They do not lay a dogmatic stencil over each text, but, with the people and on their behalf, they open themselves to the healing power of the Word of God.

THE GOSPEL IMPERATIVE

The gospel indicative contains an imperative, else it purveys cheap grace. The lonely, alcoholic man experienced the third theological movement of the sermon as the offer and challenge of integration. I believe that in order to avoid confusion we do well to use other words than "law" in giving substance to that imperative. Christ is both the end *(telos)* of the law (Rom. 10:4) and the essence of a new, comprehensive law (I Cor. 9:21), just as he is the "something greater than the temple" (Matt. 12:6) and the embodiment of the "new covenant" (Luke 22:20). But in this new situation *we* do not do the law; what the law ordains is fulfilled *in* us (Rom. 8:4). In Christ we do not return to the obligations of the law with heavier ammunition. Rather, we walk by "the law of the Spirit of life in Christ" (Rom. 8:2). What stood over me, pointing its finger at me, saying, "This you have done; this you have left undone," has been fulfilled. He who accomplished this now dwells in and among his people, fulfilling in them expressions of love that both include and surpass the requirements of the law. The Christian life is not a simple matter of exchanging an external law for an internal one (i.e., swapping a demanding statute for a nagging conscience), but of exchanging the extrinsic demand for the indwelling Christ. Life in Christ covers much of the same ground as life under the law—but is motivated by a different Spirit and directed toward a different end.

The law functions in three ways. (1) Theologically, its demands show us our sinfulness and great distance from God. (2) Politically, the law is given by God to people for the purpose of limiting evil and keeping order in society. (3) Pedagogically, the law provides guidance, or a "form" for living out the Christian faith. All are valid emphases, but because the first (theological) use of the law also permeates the other two, the Christian life of good works is better described in terms of discipleship, walking in the Spirit, or new obedience to the divine command. Christian exhortations to do the law may be misunderstood to signal a return to bondage. To those Christians who had struggled free of the law's regulations only to yearn for the security they afforded, Paul wrote, "For freedom Christ has set us free; stand fast therefore, and do not submit again to a yoke of slavery" (Gal. 5:1).

THE CORRELATION OF LAW AND GOSPEL

So far we have focused on the *distinction* between law and gospel. The preacher's method also requires their *correlation*. Great theologians such as Bonhoeffer, Tillich, and Bultmann have sought to express the gospel in the language of the secular, the psychoanalytic, and the existential, respectively. Their successes in correlating answer to question have not superseded the biblical categories, but have supplemented them and highlighted their importance. Our goals in preaching are more modest. We do not necessarily seek novel expressions of the gospel, but we do seek accurate and biblical correlations of God's answer to human problems. In the partnership of law and gospel we discover the many faces of sin and also the many shapes of God's good news. We have space for only a few of the biblical correlatives.

Guilt—Justification. Enlightened "modern man" has ceased to ask the medieval question, How may I find a gracious God? now that a sense of guilt has been unmasked for the neurosis it is. A mixed chorus of theologians and pop-psychologists has repeated this refrain with such regularity that we almost believe it. But irreligious as well as religious people continue to labor under a heavy burden of authentic guilt for which the many psycho-self-help books and programs are cruel hoaxes. The tormented young preacher in Flannery O'Connor's *Wise Blood* tries to escape his guilt with a show of bravado: "Nobody with a good car needs to be justified." But it will not work. The gospel of justification does away with two contemporary fictions: that God has quit judging sin; and that men and women find peace by learning how to feel good about themselves. Justification draws its power from God, who, despite all evidence to the contrary, declares us right in his sight. This he does simply by looking at us through Christ-colored eyes. "How is it with you and my son?" he asks. Only then does the scramble for self-justification end and the life of doing justice begin.

Debt—Forgiveness. During the Reformation era, "forgiveness" was the shorthand term for the gospel. Like justification it only works where there is a conscious sense of injury or guilt. Forgiveness implies more than human or divine forgetfulness. It cancels old debts and creates new relationships. The wounds of the unforgiven usually fester in the family: children have unfinished business with their parents; divorced men and women are beginning, willy-nilly, new lives without concluding the old; families maintain traditions of strife and ill-will. Many churches focus on families without ever ministering to the pain of the unforgiven and unforgiving that lives even in "the best of families." The danger here is that the anxious preacher, like the anxious counselor, will prescribe forgiveness too quickly and pronounce absolution too easily before the source of the symptoms is revealed.

Embattled—Victorious. In Christ's resurrection, Paul says, "he disarmed the principalities and powers and made a public example of them" (Col. 2:15). By demythologizing the powers and relating them to food taboos, drink, and other religious observances (v. 16), Paul provides a model for our preaching. Like Gulliver in the Land of Lilliput, our body of Christ, the church, is tied down in thralldom to economic, political, cultural, and institutional powers. We agree with Paul, but only in a perverse sense: "You are not your own!" My destiny is ruled by the fate of General Motors, the Pentagon, Mobil Oil, the F.D.A., the New York Stock Exchange, and other powers too dark and numerous to mention. Add to these the petty tyrannies of pride and pleasure and the absolute hegemony of death, and I am not ashamed to repeat Paul's cry, "Wretched man that I am! Who will deliver me from this body of death?" We preach *Christus Victor,* not to erase the powers, but to disarm them and rob them of their ultimate significance in our lives. Although they continue to menace us, they are shorn of their *exousia.* Proper correlation of law and gospel means that it is no good addressing the powers with an insufficient gospel or offering the "gentle Jesus" to those enslaved as by a "strong man, fully armed" (Luke 11:21).

Old Creation—New Creation. The old creation is ruled by sin, death, and Satan. It groans as it awaits its redemption. The inexorable "wasting away" (II Cor. 4:16) links humanity and nature. The forty pushups have been reduced to nine and a half, and the three miles of jogging to a brisk walk on the beach. And mothers who were once so supple, bending a thousand times a day over children, now find it inconvenient to bend and stoop. One of the pain-reliever commercials puts the question precisely, "Do you ever have that tired and run-down feeling?" And we, with the whole creation, say, Yes indeed! Listen to our fellows in all forms of war with one another; listen to the last shrieks of endangered species; listen to the brooding stillness of the late Great Lakes, and all together we can hear the travail of creation. Although there are many satisfactions in aging, there is also the burden of growing old in a hyped-up society that idolizes youth, despises old age, and denies death. In Christ we not only *feel* like new people, which is the promise of every sleeping tablet and laxative on the counter, but we *are* new people in a way that defeats the desperateness of the old creation. The eighth day of creation began on Easter morning when God reversed the old world's terminal course. And the new creation that, through baptism into Christ, God has begun in us, he promises to extend to the dead lakes, littered highways, wasted cities, and all else our hands have touched.

SEVEN CONFUSIONS OF LAW AND GOSPEL

1. *The Mechanical Application of Law and Gospel.* There is a two-fold danger at work here. One is that we lay the same stencil over every text, asking, Where is the law and gospel? rather than, What is God saying to his people? This rigid approach assures the congregation of an explication of judgment and grace whether this particular text offers it or not. The second danger is gospel pragmatism. Its question is, What problem needs solving today? Certainly the good news is addressed to a bad situation, but it cannot be bent to fit the situation. A specific human need should not determine the gospel's agenda. It is, as W. D. Davies reminds us, "the gospel of the glory of God,"[11] which celebrates its own majesty and creates its own agenda.

2. *Grace Without Judgment.* Gospel without law poses two dangers. It minimizes that *from* which we have been saved and overlooks that *for* which we have been saved. The real error in minimizing the powers of law, sin, death, and Satan is that such an approach distorts the nature of God and cheapens his act of redemption. The Lord of hosts who battled evil all the way to the cross becomes an elder statesman who hasn't visited the troops in years. All he requires is a vaguely religious attitude called "belief," in exchange for which all other responsibilities and works of love are rendered superfluous. Grace without judgment lives in a make-

believe world without evil. Its God shuns "dirty politics," avoids hospitals and prisons, and stands speechless in cemeteries.

3. *Judgment Without Grace.* The incessant launching of lightning bolts from the pulpit gives God a bad name. It exalts what the Reformers called his "alien work," that of condemnation, to a position of unwarranted superiority. This kind of preaching tries to accomplish with the law what only the gospel can do. It scares the hell out of people, but fails to scare them into heaven. Judgment without grace has contributed to these entries in *Webster's Third New International Dictionary*: Preach = "to exhort in an officious or tiresome manner" and Sermon = "an annoying harangue." When it falls upon receptive hearts, the preaching of judgment without grace produces sheer terror.

4. *Preoccupation with Analysis.* When Reuel Howe interviewed laypeople about preaching, one of the most frequently aired complaints was that sermons are long on analysis and short on solution. One layman asked, "Why do you give eighteen minutes to an analysis of man's need for the gospel and only two minutes on the gospel in relation to the need?"[12] This may be a by-product of living in an analytic age, but I prefer to think of it as a sinful failure of nerve. We have come to enjoy the problematics of modern life, and preachers, if they don't catch themselves, may even revel in the "human predicament." To an over-refined analysis, the preacher may add, if there is enough time, a gospel cliché ("Jesus died for your sins") or a gospel so abbreviated, simplistic, or unreal that it leaves the problems unanswered. The result of this preaching is frustration.

5. *Moralism.* In the intersection of law and gospel the hearer is confronted with issues of death and life that transform the sermon into a moment of meaning. It is here at this mathematical point that the sermon takes on eschatological importance. That most sermons do not seem eschatologically important, or even important, is due less to the bullying, hell-and-damnation preaching of judgment than it is to the bully's sneaky little brother, moralism. Moralism holds up the virtues, be they yesterday's piety, courtesy, and cleanliness, or today's openness, frankness, and freedom, and makes

a deadly transposition. Instead of offering its list of virtues as possible goals or consequences of the gospel, moralism subtly *prescribes* them as the *means* by which the grace of God is apprehended. Even faith is not immune to this subtle confusion of law and gospel. Moralism confuses exhortations to faith ("We all need to return to the bedrock of belief!") with faith itself; with the result that faith, as the open hand that grasps the gift, is preached as a *work* and is added to moralism's checklist of virtues.

In a letter to John Adams, Thomas Jefferson suggested that once the more offensive portions of the New Testament are excised, "There will be found remaining the most sublime and benevolent code of morals which has ever been offered to man."[13] Moralism preaches the Christian virtues without Christ-the-core, and when the congregation asks, "To whom shall we turn to become such people?" moralism offers for our imitation "Jesus Man of Genius" (J. Middleton Murry) or "The Greatest Possibility Thinker That [sic] Ever Lived."

I tell my students that at least half the sermons I read are moralistic. These sermons usually preach Jesus-our-example and think that by mentioning his good behavior they have preached the gospel. The moralistic reading of Philippians 2, for example, discerns a model for modesty rather than ministry, and focuses on the humility rather than the humiliation of Jesus. The parable of the lost coin yields a model for human persistence, and the Good Samaritan is resurrected annually for Race Relations Sunday. Similarly, the Sermon on the Mount, now lifted from its eschatological setting, becomes a list of precepts for Christians.[14] Example and precept, even when it is Christ's ultimate example of sacrifice, do not constitute good news. For as long as Christ's character, ministry, or sacrifice are held up to me as examples to be emulated, I am in the position of the little brother who is sick to death of hearing his mother say, "Why can't you be like your older sister?" However, when Jesus is preached as *prototype* rather than model,[15] the congregation is not thrown back upon its own powers of imitation, but it is fueled by a gospel which creates of its own truth faithful sons and daughters.

Finally, moralism isolates a single human quality, gratitude, and makes it the motive for a life of discipleship. Certainly, thanksgiving plays a major part in the lives of Christians, but human gratitude forms a shaky bridge between God's action in Christ and the new obedience of the Christian life. Here again, moralism sells the gospel short by failing to see that the gospel itself ("faith active in love") contains the seeds of its own performance.

Moralism, as I said, is sneaky, because it associates itself so closely with the truth, even biblical truth. Its chief hermeneutical assumption is an homogenized Bible in which all texts are equally important to the spiritual health of the reader. The Bible becomes a kind of Yellow Pages, or religious almanac, whose interminable lists of duties and consolations are not infrequently found pasted in Gideon Bibles. To what end? To the end that all bases be covered and every conceivable human dilemma, from acedia to zestlessness, be solved by a perfectly clear scriptural directive. Its aim is not security in Christ, but security from Christ and his terrible freedom. Whenever the preacher is tempted to absorb law into gospel or to preach reliance on something other than God's indicative work, the Lord himself exposes this "other's" ghastly consequences: death in the safe arms of the law.

6. *Preaching About the Gospel.* Preaching about Christianity, grace, the gospel, or the Christian life-style without offering the benefits of Christ is like speaking about food to a starving person. True preaching does not discourse on the gospel, but offers it to all in need. Another variation on this theme could be called text fundamentalism. After several years in an academic environment, theological students and teachers start preaching *about* the text rather than letting God preach through the text. The pericope is isolated from its broader context in the gospel and given supreme value in its own right. Speaking of this text's concepts and that text's understanding, interpreters forget that through these words God is addressing his people. In his lectures on homiletics given to seminarians in the Confessing Church, Dietrich Bonhoeffer challenged the students to "see if you can't say 'God says' where you would like to say, 'the Apostle John says.' "[16] Whether in a seminary

classroom, or a parish Bible circle, or a lectionary study group, text fundamentalism often aggressively venerates the Bible, but overlooks the dynamic character of its central message.

7. *Preaching the Gospel in a Law-Tone.* The final form of confusion has to do with sermon delivery. To paraphrase Paul, "Only let your manner of delivery be worthy of the gospel." Our society venerates anybody who can control a crowd. "Give 'em hell, Harry!" can turn on a politician or a preacher. Sometimes this failure to assimilate the grace of God and to take seriously its implications for public speech causes us to announce the good news in a manner befitting judgment. As Henry Mitchell is fond of saying: white radio preachers sound "fiery mad," while black-culture preachers tend to be "fiery glad." They save their energy for the gospel. Those heavy salvos we set off at human sin too often echo in our proclamation of the good news, with the result that the person in the pew hears, "God is love—and by God you'd better believe it!" If we can be fiery mad about sin, then with an even greater sense of vibrancy and passion we can be fiery glad about salvation.

John the Evangelist said of his work, "These are written that you may believe that Jesus is the Christ, the Son of God, and that believing you may have life in his name" (John 20:31). What he said of his labors, may all preachers say of theirs. We do not *balance* law and gospel for aesthetically pleasing effects. By the Spirit's help, we rightly *divide* them so that in our sermons, and in the lives of those who hear them, God's grace may overshadow and defeat his judgment, just as it did long ago in the faithful ministry of his Son. We preach life and death—with the advantage to life.

IV. PREACHING AS THE WORD OF GOD

When all was still, and it was midnight, thine almighty
Word, O Lord, descended from the royal throne.
                         Introit for the Sunday after Christmas

People listen to preaching only when they are convinced that it is
the Word of God. Before anyone could explain to him *how* or *why*
the sermon is the Word of God, the lonely man, discussed in chapter
3, heard the sermon and accepted it as such. Preaching works before
it is fully understood. Having seen the Word in action, we now
return to a theological rationale for its truth and power. In doing so I
shall try to avoid the usual hyperbole that attends Word-of-God-talk
(here I am thinking of Barth and the Barthians) in which the Word
takes on such mystic and objective properties that it fails to keep
touch with reality, especially the mundane realities of inept
preachers and recalcitrant listeners. I shall also keep my distance
from those theologies of the Word (represented by Ebeling and the
New Hermeneutic) which swallow up sacred events and church
history by subsuming all under the history of the Word. The forest of
studies on "the Word of God" and the elasticity of the concept itself
make it necessary for us to sample the literature selectively and to
join the conversation only where it will clarify the relationship of the
Word of God and preaching.

THE ORAL-AURAL WORD

If someone says "word," most of you will "see" the image of a typed or printed symbol. Our cultural perception has so long been dominated by the visual—script, print, electronic image—that from time to time voices are needed to remind us that the visual words we see are representations of a more fundamental and primal reality, namely, the word as sound. Words are for hearing. This truism has been recalled for us and its implications developed by Walter Ong in his seminal work, *The Presence of the Word*, and its sequel, *Interfaces of the Word*.[1]

Primary orality, by which Father Ong means the orality of a culture that has never known writing, afforded humankind a sense of unity technological creatures find difficult to appreciate or even imagine.

> The psyche in a culture innocent of writing knows by a kind of empathetic identification of knower and known, in which the object of knowledge and the total being of the knower enter into a kind of fusion, in a way which literate cultures would typically find unsatisfyingly vague and garbled and somehow too intense and participatory. To personalities shaped by literacy, oral folk often appear curiously unprogramed, not set off against their physical environment, given simply to soaking up existence, unresponsive to abstract demands such as a "job" that entails commitment to routines organized in accordance with abstract clock time.[2]

Although this kind of culture has its obvious problems and can never be thought of as paradisal, its original unity was as real and natural as that of mother and child (mother-tongue), and its reorientation to the eye has worked as a psychological and cultural brake on the spontaneous rhythm and flow of oral discourse.

The end of the old culture is not as easily determined as the date of the invention of the printing press, telegraph, radio, or computer. Oral-aural methods of discourse, performance, and education persisted well into the era of writing and continue to flourish in illiterate societies today. Birger Gerhardsson has demonstrated the persistence of the oral in the context of rabbinic education and the

transmission of the gospel. Concerning the production of written
literature, he reminds us that

> we are far too apt to forget that the literary works of Antiquity were not
> intended for readers sitting in quiet seclusion and leafing through rapidly
> produced and rapidly obsolete publications. In the first place, the greater
> part of the ancient literature is intended for the ears as much as, if not
> more than, the eyes. Words were meant to *sound*; authors wrote works
> which were meant to be read aloud.[3]

In a well-known passage of *The Confessions* (6:3), Augustine records
his amazement at finding Ambrose reading silently!

With the invention of the moveable-type printing press, the
Renaissance began to overcome its distrust of the written word. With
Descartes, solitary thinking was elevated over dialectical discourse,
and in seventeenth-century English thinkers such as Locke and
Hobbes human understanding was modeled exclusively (and
crudely) after sight.[4] Our electronic culture—telegraph, telephone,
radio, television, computer, etc.—may signal, if not a *return* to
oral-aural ways, certainly a *revitalization* of them built upon a
still-dominant visual, typographic mindset. For all its faults,
television re-creates the sense of participation and immediacy that
characterized preliterate societies. But it also fosters a new kind of
isolation, that of the individual viewer before the tube, which is
foreign to an oral-aural culture, and it contributes to that falsifying
and dulling of reality (Fred Allen called television "chewing gum for
the eyes") that makes preaching to the "real world" more difficult.

Although the sound produced by the spoken word is the most
evanescent of sense stimuli, it is the most alive and real of all. The
psychological effect of the living voice is the creation of a sense of
presence and power; for the living voice, as opposed to canned
electronic productions and the lifelessness of print on a page, is *now*
in active production.[5] There is no comparison between a film of the
National Theatre's *Merchant of Venice* with Laurence Olivier, and
the live performance. In the live performance, the actor's power is
immeasurably greater. When Olivier as Shylock is led off at the end
for his enforced baptism, he emits a cry of anguish so penetratingly

symbolic of all that Shakespeare was about in the play, that the audience almost forgets to breathe in its effort to become one with the character. For all the talk of word-event in post-Bultmannian circles, it is here, in the active production of sound, that deep calls unto deep and the living, resonant word becomes an "event."

The living voice, with its capacity for variation of pitch, rate, and force, makes possible a level of clarity unknown to written forms of communication. Reading and television make us spectators from the outside, but sound is the key to interiority.[6] The class may scrutinize me, the new professor, as long as it wishes, but nothing of who I am is revealed until I open my mouth and speak. What is more revealing than language? The most intimate gestures and acts of love may become impersonal, mechanical exercises unless interpreted and completed by words. Who has not submitted to a thorough medical examination without yearning for some humanizing word—even small talk!—to dull the keenness of the visual and tactile sciences.

At a more profound level, speech creates the kind of communication that not only conveys information, but evokes response. That response begins in the silence of the hearer's or the congregation's expectation and its readiness to ascribe authority to the speaker.[7] When that condition is met, listener and speaker have formed a partnership, the effects of which in the listener may be observed and even documented. The hearer (or congregation) hears the noise of sounds, vowels. He inwardly reproduces the speaker's consonants, registers completed words, sentences, phrases, and recalls their conceptual meaning. Simultaneously with this cognitive work, the listener begins to reenact the emotion behind the phrases and is moved to decision or action. The hearer leaves with the words, as well as the meanings, emotions, and decisions behind them, but ultimately gets the words out of his system—forgets them. "The news is good news for him, when he finally can forget about it because he has done something about it, and lives on. To forget a thing which we learned before we remembered or felt or acted would be wrong. Never to forget anything is an obsession. There is a time for memory as well as forgetting."[8] The lonely man we considered in chapter 3 ultimately forgot the words—they were never meant to be remembered—but internalized and enacted the dialectic conveyed in them.

FAITH COMES BY HEARING

When the Word of God broke into the silence of the world, it came as a word of preaching. It fell among people still living in two worlds, the world of the book in whose pages *words* of God might be preserved, and the age of the living Word in whose transmission the *power* of God might be experienced. Jesus wrote nothing—except a few words in the dust. He was a voice, not a penman; a herald, not a scribe;[9] whose key signature to all he taught and proclaimed was, "He who has ears to hear, let him hear." Before his gospel was a doctrine, a book, a system, or an imprimatur for civilization, it was an oral message. Paul, who was something of a reluctant writer himself, says, "And we also thank God constantly for this, that when you received the word of God which you heard from us, you accepted it not as the word of men but as what it really is, the word of God, which is at work in you believers" (I Thess. 2:13). "The word is near you, on your lips and in your heart (that is, the word of faith which we preach)" (Rom. 10:8). Again, "That word is the good news which was preached to you" (I Peter 1:25*b*). In the book of Acts, where "Word of God" is a technical term for the proclaimed gospel, we read that this message from God "increased" (6:2), "grew and multiplied" (12:24), and "prevailed mightily" (19:20). These and similar passages led Luther to the much-quoted remark, "Faith is an acoustical affair." "Stick your eyes in your ears," he counseled. "He who will not take hold with his ears but wants to look with his eyes is lost."[10] His general disparagement of a written gospel, to which I referred in chapter 1, reflects an understanding of how the kerygma was meant to work, and anticipates, with no little sophistication, modern rediscoveries of the psychological depth and power of the aurally received word.

The Christian "Word of God" (*o logos tou theou*) retains the dynamic and performative qualities of the Hebrew *dabar*. Without buying the etymological speculation concerning *dabar* (so thoroughly criticized by James Barr in *The Semantics of Biblical Language*), we may say that, for the Semite, "Word of God" connotes a creating and shaping of external reality.[11] What God says, goes. " 'Let there be light,' and there was light." The psalmist shows the perfect connection between God's words and his works:

> For the word of the Lord is upright;
> and all his work is done in faithfulness. . . .
>
> For he spoke, and it came to be;
> he commanded, and it stood forth (Ps. 33:4*a*, 9).

No one can see God and live, but he may be known in his speaking. In contrast to the God who speaks, the gods of neighboring tribes are mute and their images dumb.[12]

> Their idols are like scarecrows in
> a cucumber field,
> and they cannot speak (Jer. 10:5*a*).

The Semite word has power and permanence. Every Sunday school child asks why, when Isaac discovered that he had spoken a blessing over the wrong child, he did not simply "take it back." He could not; the word spoken became the deed done. In the New Testament, Jesus' word carries that kind of performative authority—not only in its reliance upon the sacred texts, but in its power to change lives and create new situations. As Bultmann has said, "His works are his words [and] his words are his works."[13] To a deaf man he said, "Be opened"; to the corpse of a child, "Little girl, I say to you, arise"; to some scribes he posed the problematic, "Which is easier, to say, 'Your sins are forgiven,' or to say, 'Rise and walk'?" And to a storm he said, "Peace! Be still!"

Because it is God who speaks, and the Holy Spirit who attends the Word, those who preach, teach, and give testimony do so with the assurance that the Word's effective power is not diminished. The preacher or prophet is simply given God's words, a gift that overcomes the hesitancy and inarticulateness of the prophet. God not only imparts the truth, but he also touches the prophet's mouth, as in Jeremiah and Isaiah, to empower the delivery of the truth. So the greatest of God's representatives in the Old Testament, Moses, seems to have had a speech impediment. To Moses' reasonable protestations of ineloquence, God answers with an offer so comprehensive that it covers the production and enunciation of the divine words: "Who has made man's mouth? . . . Now therefore go, and I will be with your mouth and teach you what you shall speak" (Ex. 4:11a-12). So also in the New Testament God intervenes with new tongues on Pentecost, creating a Babel-in-reverse and changing simple fisherfolk into proclaimers of the Word. Even *with* the Spirit, public speaking does not seem to have been Paul's strong suit. The cultured despisers of his day, among whom rhetorical elegance was greatly admired, gave the apostle some frightful pulpit reviews: "For they say, 'His letters are weighty and strong, but his bodily presence is weak, and his speech of no account' "(II Cor. 10:10). Paul knew that the preacher is but a steward, mouthpiece, witness, emissary, slave, and earthen vessel, but by virtue of the mystery over which he is *oikonomos*, the message for which he is *kerux*, the event to which he is *martus*, the Lord from whom he is *apostolos*, and the master to whom he is *doulos*, he boldly claims yet another title: *sunergos theou*, God's partner. With Paul, every preacher knows that the Word will work, and confidently owns the promise of God.

> For as the rain and the snow come down from heaven,
> and return not thither but water the earth,
> making it bring forth and sprout, giving seed to the sower
> and bread to the eater, so shall my word be that goes forth
> from my mouth; it shall not return to me empty,
> but it shall accomplish that which I purpose, and prosper
> in the thing for which I sent it (Isa. 55:10-11).

To preach the Word of God also means to tell the truth about God. The Greek, dianoetic concept of *logos* reminds us that preaching is a rational organization of what Luke called "the facts about Jesus" (Acts 18:25 NEB). It is a story that, in its telling, will evoke no less care and craftsmanship on the part of the preacher than it did in the meticulously researched and orderly narrative of the evangelist (Luke 1:1-4). With Paul (as in I Cor. 15:1 ff.) the preacher will examine the "terms" in which the gospel is transmitted, so that the Word of God as a rationally organized *traditum* can arrive intact. Even in this model of organized transmission, the memory of oral preaching lies very near the surface. It is quite different in the Pastoral Epistles, however, where we see the Hebrew dynamic giving way to the Greek dianoetic in the writers' concern to certify and guard the Word of God. This aspect of the church's understanding of the Word need not be read as a weakening, for just as the Hebrew dynamic energized the Word, so the Greek dianoetic channeled that flow of energy, and together they have given vitality to the church's proclamation.

JESUS: PROCLAIMER AND PROCLAIMED

A cursory review of the objects of the New Testament verbs for "preach" shows how saturated with Christ that early proclamation was. Some of the objects are: Jesus, Lord Jesus, Christ, Jesus Christ as Lord, Christ crucified, Christ as raised from the dead, Jesus and the resurrection, good news about the Kingdom, Jesus as the Son of God, the gospel of God, Word of the Lord, the forgiveness of sins, and Christ in you—the hope of glory. The one who had said of his own preaching ministry, "That is why I came out" (Mark 1:38*b*), had become the content of his church's proclamation.

But the church's preaching was more intimately related to Jesus than a message is to its content. He was the very expression of the Father, the actively produced sound which in its fidelity to its source tells the truth about the Father and in its obedience does his will on earth. The writer to the Hebrews sums up all that the Word can mean when, with a single declarative sentence, the subject, God, utters his final predicate: "In many and various ways God spoke of old to our fathers by the prophets; but in these last days he has spoken to us by a Son, whom he appointed the heir of all things, through whom also he created the world" (Heb. 1:1-2).

The Hebrews passage anticipates the themes of the prologue to the

Gospel of John, but where John's account focuses on the static concept of *logos*, the writer of Hebrews catches the dynamic action of speaking in the Semitic sense in which no distinction is made between the word and the person who utters it. What John adds is the vivid imagery of the Word made flesh and the sense of commitment in that Word's encampment with human beings (1:14). Like God's original creative Word, his final word in Christ binds and commits him to his creation. God's self-expression is not a virtuoso display of power, or even revelation (contra Barth), but from his first to his final word he has spoken in love, and in these last days has disclosed himself as

> The word within a word, unable to speak a word
> Swaddled with darkness. . . .[14]

To that spoken Word, humanity is created to respond and *re*created to respond in love.

So identified is Jesus the Word with the word of preaching, that the one proclaimed once again becomes the proclaimer. Insofar as preaching rearticulates the saving themes and offers the life of God in Christ, it is Jesus himself who is the preacher, blessing our sermons with his presence. Martin Kähler's famous statement was, "The real Christ is the preached Christ," an edict that effectively severed proclamation from the historical incarnation and ministry of Jesus. In contrast, Christian preaching continues the ministry of Jesus just as surely as it continues the ministry of the apostles. This preaching refuses to relinquish the mighty acts of God in Christ to the impenetrable mists of history (where Schweitzer's *Quest* left off), but continues to describe, recite, and celebrate the works as prerequisites for preaching. For the God who lives today must also be proclaimed as the God who lived yesterday; the God of the future must have a past.[15] Barth is emphatic about this when he says that preaching does not occur as a spiritual event (or what some theologians have called a word-event), but only in continuity with the fleshly Christ. Bonhoeffer, too, stresses the incarnation when he insists, "The proclaimed word is the Christ bearing human nature."[16] Catholic doctrine knows that the risen and ascended Christ maintains his human nature. He dwells among his people, and his servants, such as Paul, carry in their bodies the death and life of Jesus so that his form of the truly human might eventually gain a greater measure of recognition throughout the whole body of the church. The human nature of Christ in our proclamation is most apparent in the folly of preaching, as men and women struggle within the limitations of language to "name the whirlwind." The crucified Christ is himself the source of this folly and the cause of our preaching's worldly failures. With Paul on Mars Hill we uncover the long-hidden God, only to reveal, presto, a beat-up and bleeding Jew, and our sophisticated audiences clear their throats nervously and move on. The divine nature of Christ is most apparent in the glory of preaching, which, paradoxically, rests squarely upon the folly of the cross. But to those who are determined to know nothing but the cross and to accept its folly as the highest wisdom (I Cor. 1:22-25), God issues a call and invitation to partnership. The glory of preaching consists in the human stewardship of these mysteries of God, a stewardship that is given in grace and accepted by the preacher in humility and childlike trust.

THE WRITTEN WORD OF SCRIPTURE

It is as difficult to find ministers who are against biblical preaching as it is to find biblical preaching. Everyone is for it, yet there is little agreement on the interpretation and authority of Scripture among those who profess to preach it, and by most contemporary assessments of the state of the art, biblical preaching (by which I mean more than preaching with an open Bible on the pulpit) is in deep trouble. The preacher may begin with a short piece on the profundity of the Bible's "timeless truths," much in the way a reviewer praises a book or a film before burying it, but it soon becomes clear that in this sermon the Bible will serve only as background Muzak for the preacher's own ideas. We cannot pause to describe the methods of biblical preaching, but we must understand why the Bible is essential to the church's proclamation. For many it is enough to say that, through the canonical books of the Old and

New Testaments, God speaks. Period. But for the preacher, who interprets and proclaims the church's book to both church and world, Leander Keck adds a compelling reason: "Apart from serious engagement with the Bible there is simply no way of testing whether what seems like good news in a given era is in fact the gospel."[17] The Bible is the test of preaching.

As we have seen in chapter 2, the risen Christ called forth preaching; and preaching, in its broad sense as proclamation, transformed the followers of Jesus and reconstituted them as the church. Through the power of this word of proclamation thousands of people were baptized, received the Holy Spirit, and were added to the body of believers, so that the church grew in stature and in favor with God and man. Although early Christian preaching relied heavily on the Old Testament scriptures, the catechetical, liturgical, and missionary needs of the church were such that it was necessary to capture the oral message in written form. While it is proper to say that the church created the canon to norm its proclamation, it is more accurate to say that the gospel itself, through its various oral modalities and uses in the church, created the canon, and that the church merely recognized it. In its recognition and acceptance of the canon the church continues to differentiate the work of the Spirit in all churchly activity, including preaching, from the Spirit's role in the production of the New Testament and the formation of the canon. It is the same Spirit who works in all, but in the Scriptures, God was establishing a permanent witness to Christ and a definitive exposition of the gospel.

Thus, at a series of points early in its history, the church made frozen sections of the tradition which, until Christians also became "people of the book," had been a surging, and even volatile, force within the church.[18] The church bound itself to the Book not because of its inspiration, inerrancy, perspicuity, unity, efficacy, or any of the other attributes later woven into Protestant orthodoxy's "doctrine of the Holy Scriptures," but for the permanency of its truth, its usefulness in serving the needs that had originally summoned it into existence, and its apostolicity. This last simply means that the church wanted a book written by committed insiders, and not by informed observers, innocent bystanders, or antiquity's equivalent of sociologists of religion. Thus there was a time when the book was not, when the oral gospel could be differentiated from the collections of sayings and narratives which had not yet found a home in a literary gospel and achieved canonical status. But in the canon that distinction is done away with forever. As important as the history of the precanonical forms is to the interpretation of the text, the church steadfastly recognizes only the canonical text as the source and norm of its doctrine, preaching, and practice.

The authority of the Bible is a circle. Various points on the circle might be labeled inspiration, antiquity, clarity, beauty, truthfulness, divine authorship, and gospel. To one, the Bible's authority is bound up with inspiration; to another, its divine authorship; to yet another, the gospel. While most of the points in the circle constitute appropriate reasons for the believer to accept the authority of Scripture, it is finally the gospel that enables the lector, having read the appointed lessons, to elevate the Bible and say, "The Word of the Lord."

Gospel and Scripture ought not to be divided or played off against each other. The noetic, informational skeleton of the New Testament can no more be separated from its dynamic, evangelical heart than Christ's human nature can be separated from the divine. Both are essential to salvation. Perhaps this is why most attempts to peel away the skin in order to get at the pure kerygma, that is, a kerygma acceptable to contemporary ethical, scientific, or political standards, so often result in a net loss of biblical truth. In its reduced or "purified" form the biblical message has been rendered unrecognizable to the faithful and deprived of its power to attract and convert the nonbeliever. The believer instinctively knows that there is more to the gospel than "authenticity," "liberation," or an "open future"; and the nonbeliever, hearing these thin replications of his own hopes and dreams, decides to keep what he has. Jesus once chided his opponents for knowing neither the Scriptures nor the power of God (Matt. 22:29); on another occasion he criticized those who separate the power of God from the Scriptures (John 5:39). What the oral gospel has communicated to the written word is, miraculously, the dynamic power of the Word to work repentance and to create faith and obedience. John's daring statement of purpose for his *book* is that which was previously attributable only to the *viva voce*, and would have been intelligible only in a culture still oriented to the ear. John wrote, "These are written that you may believe that Jesus is the Christ, the Son of God, and that believing you may have life in his name" (John 20:31).

By faith we accept the Bible as the Word of God and celebrate the consummation of its divine and human authorship. We preach, not the Bible, but the Christ of the Bible. Bibliolatry, said Luther, worships the cradle instead of the Christ child in it. Jesus meant the same when he said, "You study the scriptures diligently, supposing that in having them you have eternal life; yet, although their testimony points to me, you refuse to come to me for that life" (John 5:39-40 NEB). A biblical sermon is an exposition of the Scripture, which is an exposition of the gospel, which is an exposition of the life of God himself. We preach the Bible kerygmatically according to its own *raison d'être*, knowing that to do anything less is to reduce the living scriptural Word to a dead letter.

THE SERMON: WORD OF GOD

Praedicatio verbi Dei est verbum Dei. "The preaching of the Word of God is the Word of God." So spoke the Second Helvetic Confession, and so speaks much of the church today. To claim for our flatulent pronouncements the status "Word of God" may be a bit much to swallow; to fail to make that claim, however, is to forget that, as long as our frailty represents frailty *before God*, it is never absolute, for he is able to make of it what he wills.[19] It is impossible to divide sermons into Word of God and word of man, but insofar as preaching participates in the historic succession of proclamation (as Barth calls it), it is the Word of God we preach, as surely as Peter and Paul preached the Word of God. Barth adds, "For so far as proclamation really rests upon recollection of the revelation attested in the Bible and is therefore the obedient repetition of the Biblical witness, it is no less the Word of God than the Bible."[20]

The sermon is the oral Word of God. The sermon does not exist as a sermon until it is uttered. It is twice-born, as Bonhoeffer said, once in the study and once in the pulpit. It is *delivered* in the sense of the birthing that takes place after a period of prayerful and disciplined incubation; and it is delivered, as *paradosis* or *traditum*, when that which has been received is handed on. The sermon as a speaking event follows the principles and purposes appropriate to the oral word of the Lord. Although the preacher may have prepared a manuscript, the sermon, if it is to be genuinely oral-aural, will be more than a rendering of the manuscript. "Write for the ear" is good advice, but advice still conditioned by the world of print. The more oral the minister's sermon preparation, the more aural (and intelligible) will be the final product. This will undoubtedly entail simpler sermon designs, the use of formula repetition, less precision in analysis, and a return to the great preaching themes and stories of the Bible. It is no surprise that the above are characteristics of communication in preliterate societies, and it is no accident that they have appeared most clearly and successfully in the black preaching tradition.[21] The black tradition knows that language is half speaking and half listening—but active, responsive listening—and therefore has intuitively grasped the Word of God as a "speech event" long before that phrase slipped in and out of vogue.

The sermon is the Word of God for a particular time, place, and people. Books, tapes, and computers have provided us with so many kinds of "extra-mental storage arrangements" (as Ong calls them) that the purpose of preaching can today be more clearly defined in terms of its unique character as oral language. The fluid and fleeting nature of language, far from being an accidental property of preaching to be lamented, belongs to its nature; the spoken word has its fullest truth among the people between whom it flourishes, and in the moment at which it happens.[22] That is why printed sermons or, worse, "closet sermons" are almost always duds. The preacher need not worry that his or her words are not remembered, for the words are needed only so long as it takes for them to form Christ in the hearers. If the words are not forgotten, the hearer can become obsessed with them, and that obsession will veil the reality they mean to convey.

The Word of God "fitly spoken" requires a sense of timing.

Preaching endeavors to match words with situations, so that the *now* of God's summons finds its *now* in the congregation of listeners. In this vein, Rosenstock-Huessy makes an illuminating distinction. "Pseudo speech is speech which externally says the same thing as the right speech. Only, it is not told the right person in the right place and the right time. Any truth has to be said specifically. . . . The world is full of misplaced and mistimed speeches. It lives by the few speeches made at the right time in the right place."[23] An example that comes to mind is the speech delivered by Prime Minister Neville Chamberlain. He spoke a good word of "peace in our time," but at the wrong moment in history—after signing the Munich Agreement with Hitler.

The oral Word of God in the sermon bespeaks commitment. Any act of speech involves ambivalence, that is, an inner conflict between the desire to hoard the word and the desire to release it. A speech event means that the ambivalence has been temporarily solved and that the speaker is willing to engage in some measure of self-revelation. In preaching, the speaker's stakes are even higher, for the words convey ultimate realities toward which the speaker may not remain disinterested. Already, in standing to speak in the assembly, he or she has evinced courage, passion, and conviction. The preacher who lays manuscript aside and endeavors to communicate from depth to depth runs a double risk: rejection of God and rejection of self. The foolishness of the cross as well as the spiritual and intellectual limitations of the preacher are paraded across the stage of church and community. For the commitment this kind of communication requires, *love* is not too strong a word. "Do you love me? . . . Feed my sheep," Jesus said. Marriage counselors report that the most frequently heard presenting problem is, "We have a communications problem," as though it were a matter of technical difficulties like misconnected wires or trouble along the line. But when communication is understood as commitment, "communications problems" may mean love problems, for love always finds a way to communicate itself. So, forgetful of self, the preacher holds nothing back and takes whatever risks necessary in order to insure the delivery of the gospel. The power for this kind of commitment comes from no particular preaching model in the

Bible, not Peter before the Council or Paul before Agrippa, but rather from God's own commitment in "speaking" the Word made flesh, who then came and pitched his tent among us (John 1:14).

The Word of God in the sermon works. The Word of God's truth, which exposes and illumines a given situation, also has within it the power to transform that situation. This is the assurance we preachers must have, or long ago we would have accepted the conventional advice to give up on preaching or to subcontract it to the television evangelists. Even when the Word seems only to be rebounding and echoing off the sanctuary walls, we trust that the Word of God arrives at the Spirit's destination at the Spirit's appointed time. Every preacher knows this, but only by faith; he or she also knows the folly of trying to predict or trace the empirical effectiveness of Sunday's sermon in the lives of those for whom it was preached. So goes the ditty from the off-Broadway musical *The Fantasticks*:

> Plant a carrot, get a carrot,
> Not a brussels sprout.
> That's why I like vegetables:
> You know what you're about. *

How convenient if the Word worked that way. But preachers report that when confirmation of the Word's performative power does arrive, it usually comes from unexpected quarters as a response to one of the preacher's less distinguished efforts. A pedestrian Advent sermon on hope comes home to a young mother at dawn as she sits at the bedside of her sick child. A sermon on St. Bartholomew's Day, of all things, inspires some young people to take Christ into the neighborhood. A sermon on commitment to racial justice, designed to stir up the congregation, does just that, and the preacher is fired. Perhaps it is fortunate that we cannot predict the workings of the Word and the drifts of the Spirit's influence, for then we should become manipulators of the Word instead of its servants, advertisers of our own success rather than stewards of the mysteries of God.

---

*From *The Fantasticks/Celebration* by Tom Jones and Harvey Schmidt (New York: Drama Book Specialists [Publishers], 1973), pp. 74-75.

V. CHRISTIAN ANTHROPOLOGY
AND THE POSSIBILITY OF PREACHING

What a novelty! What a monster, what a chaos, what a contradiction, what a prodigy! Judge of all things, imbecile worm of the earth; depository of truth, a sink of uncertainty and error; the pride and refuse of the universe!

Pascal *Pensées* (434)

Any theology that takes the Word of God seriously must reckon with its greatest source of embarrassment: the Word must be spoken and received by sinful human beings. With the renewed interest in hermeneutics, theology has become a keen observer of its own difficulties in translation and transmission, but, like the married couple with "communication problems," it has turned a glass eye toward the theological causes of these difficulties. The many factors contributing to the hermeneutical dilemma are usually analyzed with a sense of detachment appropriate to any discipline that deals in ancient and authoritative texts. Theology rightly joins this inquiry into the possibility of preaching; but before it uncritically accepts the conclusions of the cultural anthropologists and philosophers of *Existenz*, it must reflect theologically (that is, on its own terms) upon this volatile, yet programmed, profanely sacred, paradoxical creature named *Adam* (human) and *Adamah* (earth). The revelation about humanity offers no neutral pre-understandings concerning human reason, language, history, or any other data to which a theological slant might be superadded. God is in the human picture from beginning to end. In the remainder of the fragment quoted in the epigraph, Pascal continues, "Know then, proud man, what a paradox you are to yourself. Humble yourself, weak reason; be silent, foolish nature; learn that man infinitely transcends man, and learn from your Master your true condition, of which you are ignorant. Hear God."[1] The hoary and persistent distinction between the *Image* of God, by which Irenaeus meant the capacity for reason and goodness—still intact—and the *Likeness* of God, by which he meant the prelapsarian righteousness and blessedness, was the first of many attempts to carve out a neutral territory in humanity. The most recent exercise of this distinction occurred in existentialist theology's acceptance of an anthropology that (not unlike the older natural theologies) understands the human situation almost entirely on the basis of philosophical analysis, and proceeds to introduce the revelation of Christ and his call to a new future as a kind of *deus ex machina*. Given the antitheses of humanity's relationship to God, in which the person is both friend and enemy, partner and saboteur—but always creature and child—what *is* it about this relationship that makes public speech about God both possible and impossible?

WHAT MAKES PREACHING IMPOSSIBLE

In his poetic drama *Brand*, Henrik Ibsen captures the figure of the lonely, fiercely independent prophet, whose vocation has isolated him from the society to which he is sent. From the chill darkness of the Norwegian mountain where he lives, Brand continues to preach his message of "All or Nothing" despite the deaths of his wife and child. Early in the drama, the more reasonable Ejnar warns him,

> Do not blow out the match because it smokes
> Before the lantern lights the road.
> Do not destroy the old language
> Until you have created the new.[2]

In his zeal for perfection he pulls down the old church in the village, and along with it, its old god of compromise and easy pleasures. But the people do not follow Brand, and he dies in the Ice Church high in the mountains.

Prophecy, at least *that* kind of prophecy, has died out in the land. Not only the hearers, but also the preachers of the Word are implicated in the conditions of cynicism, naturalism, banality, and unbelief which have again and again defeated and humiliated preaching. Preaching has become an impossible task, and the preacher like someone speaking into a dead microphone.[3]

Preaching and hearing is an historical activity; it is a part of the eschatological action of God which has broken into history and now lives on the "inside" of history (to borrow Collingwood's phrase). But momentous changes have taken place in this cocoon of history in which God's eschaton awaits its own rebirth, and those who are in Christ cannot remain unaffected or unimplicated.

One such change is the growing cynicism toward language. Of course, humankind has always dissembled with words; the Genesis story describes the Fall as a result of a series of lies in which the meanings of words are twisted and used for evil purposes. The misuse of language, however, contradicts its original creative potential; language, especially public speech, is an exercise in optimism, and for the religious person, it is an expression of hope. If the ancient rhetors had not believed that the quality of life in the Athenian polis could be improved, they would not have spoken, and our rhetorical tradition would be impoverished. Historically, public oratory (and preaching) thrived whenever the people believed in the perfectability of democracy or, in the case of preaching, in the urgent reality of the kingdom of God. The loss of hope in public speaking is often tied to the rise of big government and the absence of more manageable democratic forms of life. When the polis disappeared, and later when the Republic gave way to the Empire, the inventiveness of classical rhetoric finally lost out to the elocutionary art of defending the status quo.[4] In America this is also true. We begin with the Renaissance man, a Jefferson, and end with a technocrat, a manager; we begin with philosophical principles and end with statistics; we begin with democracy and end with bureaucracy. The effects of this movement on the language of a people do not have to be documented. One may open any of the works of George Orwell—or the daily newspaper—for copious illustration.

We have learned to distrust words, and rightly so. Even such words as "democracy," "perfectability," and "kingdom of God" in the above paragraph mask as much as they reveal, and no one articulates a position on any subject without flirting with ideology. The underside of democracy was slavery; the implication of perfectability was the Master Race; the vehicle for the kingdom of God was the lunatic Crusades and mass murder in the name of Jesus. Ordinary, simple words have been kidnapped and their meanings pressed into service by powers foreign to their original intent. War is now pacification, and our offensive nuclear capability is monitored by the Department of Defense. We take the lives of unborn children in the name of freedom of choice, while the abortion debate proceeds by means of a thoroughly dehumanized vocabulary—with its fetuses, tissues, and procedures—the like of which has not been heard since Swift's *A Modest Proposal*. The mass distribution of words by means of television and the publishing industry has devalued language and (literally!) denatured the world. Flashing neon words have corrupted the winding streets of mountain villages and ruined the handsome boulevards of seaside towns. Even the sky is no longer free of them. At the beach, words trailing behind airplanes crisscross the sky as man and nature conspire to advertise discotheques and remedies for athlete's foot and worse. The only mystery in all this is why we do not hate words more than we do.

That preachers should be implicated in the distrust of language is most ironical, for preaching tells of a God who creates, redeems, and sustains by a word. Preaching as an exercise in hope is, or should be, a paradigm for all forms of public discourse. In our time the cynicism toward language has become symptomatic of a larger, more global and ecumenical pessimism based on our new-found ability to abort the human venture through nuclear devices. Now, with total destruction a distinct possibility, the divine assurances have a hollow ring. The promises of Jeremiah and Isaiah notwithstanding, there is no return from the exile of nuclear self-destruction. It has become easier for preachers to reflect the agony than to project the hope. Again, under such circumstances, preaching is—impossible.

These changes in the environment of preaching have been accompanied by the discovery and grudging recognition of uncharted subterranean strata within the human animal. Christian doctrine has never minced words when addressing the sinfulness and even total depravity of human nature. When Luther finally did away with the theologically and exegetically perverse distinction between the Image and Likeness of God, he exposed the corruption of all the faculties of body and soul, especially the will and the intellect, in order to reaffirm humankind's radical reliance on God for justification. He dismissed not the unique rationality of persons, but the idea, as Thomas Aquinas had expressed it, that this faculty naturally inclines humankind toward the truth about God and peaceable life in society.[5] But even this harsh appraisal of human nature remains within the bounds of the medieval view of *humanitas*, which did not contrast human greatness with nature, but human lowliness, capacity for error, and transience with God.[6] And as long as God was there, even total depravity had its meaning and purpose, and was not without hope of redemption. In this context, preaching could still, following the classical ideal, imitate nature by adhering to the natural flow of human reasoning and by appealing to human motives as it understood them. In this ordered view of human nature, the flesh was for the spirit, just as guilt was for forgiveness, sin was for redemption, and earthly life was for heaven. On impact with Freud, the symmetry and order of human self-understanding have been permanently deranged. Appeals to human nature now have to reckon with its dark underside which bubbles with irrational conflicts and desires; indeed, the possibility of rational speech's communicating to the depths of human irrationality has been called into question. And if Freud was wrong, well, as Paul Roazen writes in "The Legend of Freud," "Any writer whose mistakes have taken this long to correct . . . is quite a figure in intellectual history."[7] The scary thing about psychoanalytic theory is not that it asks "What is man?" but that it fails to add, "that *Thou* art mindful of him." Instead, God the Father, the refuge and stay of Christian conceptions of human nature, has been replaced by god the father–figure who must eventually be slain by all his sons and daughters. Implicated at this depth, the preacher is likely to feel his call to speak a rational word of God to the human situation a futile—and impossible—task.

Whether contemporary unbelief is greater than that of other eras and generations is difficult to ascertain. The "Age of Faith" fused elements of superstition and clericalism with a hierarchical world-picture in a way contemporary religious sensibilities would find offensive and even pagan. What is certain, however, is that modern society exhibits a greater intentionality and self-consciousness in its disposal of God than did previous eras. While the premodern age postulated a God who was present and, in the context of that presence, denied him repeatedly, the present age, including contemporary religious thought, norms its life and reflection on the hidden God, the absent God, or the dead God, and proceeds to mourn his death and/or to thrash about after his presence. In this context, paradoxically, preachers seem to have more than ever to say, a chattiness that accords with Robert Funk's aphorism: "When God is silent, man becomes a gossip."[8] When the choice between belief and unbelief ceases to be an exercise of the will within a divinely designed arena and becomes instead a condition of futility hedged by science, secularism, and reductionist understandings of human nature—that is, hedged by the arena itself—preaching becomes nervous about its obligation to say "Thus says the Lord," and reflects more and more on the impossibility of its task. Preachers, who in earlier generations had identified themselves as bearers of "the eternal gospel for a changing world," now have come to understand that their timeless message no longer emerges from a cultural wellspring of faith, but swirls in the maelstrom of unbelief, and that they, like all twentieth-century men and women, are also carriers, in the sense of unwitting transmitters, of this new and godless age.

THE CONCUPISCENCE OF PREACHING

But is it possible for a Christian to be a *carrier* of modern unbelief in the sense of one who is immune to the disease which is carried? It is one thing to live silently in the shadows of a skeptical age but quite another to step into the light in order to proclaim a message toward which the speaker harbors deep and perhaps unconscious ambivalence. Experience in homiletics classes reminds us that preaching magnifies theological or vocational uncertainties tenfold. When a carrier proclaims the gospel, the preacher may be forcibly alienated from his or her own identity as a twentieth-century person, an alienation for which the German word *Selbstentfremdung*, "estrangement from self," gives the exact description. For in preaching, it is precisely this self, or what remains of it, plagued by cosmic loneliness and irrational urges and fears, that must be transcended so that God in Christ may once again become the subject, object, and verb of all our sermons. This transcending of self happens when one partly accepts its baser attributes for what they are and partly rejects them for what they have failed to become. This "I yet not I" of which we spoke in chapter 3 is joined to the Christ in repentance and hope and in him finds that integration which makes speech about God possible.

But there are shortcuts. In an effort to reduce the tension of self-estrangement, preachers may bypass the essential stages of repentance and hope. They will preach for self-gratification, out of what C. S. Lewis called need-love, or what the Christian tradition terms concupiscence. Concupiscence is lust or *eros*, not necessarily sexual, that desires to draw the whole of reality into itself. Tillich gives the examples of Nero, Don Juan, and Faust, whose insatiable desires were set not so much on power, sex, or knowledge in themselves, but on the *totality* of the conquest.[9] The concupiscence of preaching is not what Paul had in mind when he said, "For necessity is laid upon me. Woe to me if I do not preach the gospel!" (I Cor. 9:16*b*). Those who preach out of need-love never get enough of preaching. Why? Because they can never get enough of the stroking that denies or temporarily controls those terrifying aspects of the self that have not yet been recognized or transcended in Christ. So it is that when the sermon is finished, depending on audience response, such preachers either go on a high of exhilaration or crash in utter despondency. This exaggerated need for affirmation of the self turns preaching into therapy—not for the congregation, but for the preacher.

The concupiscence of preaching takes a more controlled and philosophical turn in current-day hermeneutical discussions, whose common assumption is the untenability of the subject-object dichotomy and whose common quest is the method or formula for its disappearance. From Schleiermacher to Dilthey to Heidegger to Hans-Georg Gadamer, the philosophy of hermeneutics has sought what Gadamer calls "the fusion of horizons," that is, the assimilation of the interpreter's "prejudices" or traditions into the life and horizon of the text under investigation.[10] This fusion is the necessary goal of the historian, and every historian and theologian struggles with a method of its attainment. The effort toward total participation in the historical past, which Dilthey termed "understanding," may focus on the subjectivity of the historian (as it did, for instance, in R. G. Collingwood, for whom "history" eventually came to mean that which is reenacted in the mind of the historian).[11] Or the theology of history may focus on the objectivity of history, as expressed in the work of Wolfhart Pannenberg, in which case God becomes the guarantor of universal history. Only the God who reveals himself in the totality of history makes historical knowledge possible.[12]

I have alluded to hermeneutical theory only to underline its quest for the *all* in matters of textual understanding and to remind preachers of the impossibility of the quest. For Luther, the interpreter's distance from a true understanding of God's Word was caused by human sinfulness and creatureliness.[13] To the extent that philosophical hermeneutics pushes against the limits of human creatureliness, its rhetoric—as it filters "down" to preachers in secondary sources and slogans— can create unrealistic expectations. This side of mysticism, no amount of exegesis or homiletical technique will allow preacher and hearers to cross over into another time and into another person's skin. The otherness of the past remains. The notion of invading the past in order to become contemporaneous with it gives rise to sermon titles like "A Day in Old Capernaum" and the accurate observation that the congregation that gives its pastor a trip to the Holy Land pays for it twice. The quest for the perfect sermon, in which the hearer's horizon is fused with that of an ancient text, remains a chimera and one more evidence of the concupiscence of preaching.

WHAT MAKES PREACHING POSSIBLE?

If the gulf between the interpreter and the object of interpretation is absolute, then preaching will strive, in words Adolf von Harnack applied to his science, "to get intellectual control of the object."[14] But what if the object is God? And what if God says, as he does to Job, "I will question *you*, and you shall declare to me" (Job 38:3*b*)? Are we not likely to answer with Job:

> Behold, I am of small account;
> what shall I answer thee?
> I lay my hand on my mouth.
> I have spoken once, and I will not answer;
> twice, but I will proceed no further (Job 40:4-5).

It may appear that preaching is possible because of the universals of human life—the emotions, needs, and prototypal situations—which do not change from era to era. Men and women still stand in need of prayer; despair and hope, the fear of death, broken relationships between fathers and sons—these, it may be argued, have no need of "translation." Or it may appear that humanity's powers of reasoning and language, its moral sensibilities, or any of the other qualities by which humankind is separated from the animals, serve to make preaching a viable and useful activity. But the evidence against the possibility of preaching continues to mount, and Jesus' question remains: "How can ye, being evil, speak good things?" (Matt. 12:34 KJV).

Preaching begins with hearing the voice of God. Robert Funk writes with great wisdom, "He who aspires to the enunciation of the word must first learn to hear it; and he who hears the word will have found the means to articulate it."[15] The prophet interprets his own ability to speak in the context of listening when he says,

> The Lord God has given me
> the tongue of those who are taught,
> that I may know how to sustain with a word
> him that is weary.
> Morning by morning he wakens,
> he wakens my ear
> to hear as those who are taught (Isa. 50:4).

Christian anthropology has used the term "Image of God" to describe the intimate, responsive relationship between God and humanity.[16] The Image of God is a visual concept that has long been subject to misinterpretation along the lines of, for example, Thomas Aquinas, who taught that the image referred, among other things, to man's upright stature, or Luther, who enjoyed speculating on Adam's prelapsarian mental and physical prowess. The visualism of the image, however, is misleading, for in reality it has to do with humankind's ability to listen and to name. The human animal may demonstrate its humanity by making symbols or flint axes, fire or totems; it may bury its dead, harness the animals, and paint the walls of its cave, but theologically speaking, until the creature evaluates its new proficiencies in relation to God and the needs of the tribe, the creature still has an Image problem.

Living in the Image of God does not represent yet another function for humankind, *homo religiosus*, to be included under a larger category of reflective consciousness. Nor do I promote the Image of God as the true measure of man only because science is showing us every day that it can duplicate in the laboratory or discover in the animal world the functional equivalents of skills previously limited by definition to humans. The Image transcends the subhuman and human proficiencies that contribute to the evolution of human consciousness, for its speech activity is derived from God and is sustained in awareness of him. Originally, speech became truly human when it was returned directly to God in worship or indirectly to him in love for the community. Even the three divisions of consciousness made popular by St. Augustine cannot in themselves form the true nature of humankind. For if memory, will, and mind, Luther warned, constitute the Image of God, then Satan also possesses God's Image.

The mark of God's Image is answerability, or its equivalent, responsibility in love. The self which the person discovers in reflection is not merely the outcome of physical or economic needs, but is what C. S. Lewis called "the permanent bed" that enables humanity to evaluate successive needs and experiences while maintaining its own identity. Humanity discovers this "I" only when it is addressed by God as a "Thou."[17] *There* is the power of words! *There* is the call to be answered! Since this accountability is directed to the infinite God, the person's use of words takes on an open transcendence that may be distinguished from the sophisticated signals of the higher mammals and even from human symbols, which retain a kind of "lower case" transcendence.

The Image of God consists not only in the ability to make words, but, more fully, in the person's relationship with the Word made flesh, who is the foremost expression, not only of God's reason, but of his love. "So," concludes Thomas Aquinas, "the divine image should be looked for in man in terms of the word conceived out of awareness of God, and of the love flowing from that."[18] The rationality that characterizes the divine and human word procession is therefore incomplete without the accompanying love that wills the creation, the communication of words, and the gift of relationship that puts humankind in touch with the infinite.

We do not seek the Image of God by speculating on the constitution of the first human creature or tribe. The New Testament has shown a better way by revealing the perfection of the Image to whom humanity turns for the confirmation of its calling and justification by God. The primal Word was in the beginning and continues to brood over the brokenness of the divine-human relationship, symbolized in Genesis by the serpent's duplicity with words and the confusion at Babel, and in the Gospel of John by the world's perverse refusal to hear the words of the Word. Only Jesus reveals the true meaning of the Image of God. By living in unity with God he at once revealed humanity's distance from the Father and its need for restoration. In his perfect relationship to God and in his historical brotherhood with humanity, Jesus mediates the reunion of God and his creatures and exalts the Image beyond the simplicity of its origins to that into which we are changed, from glory to glory, by the Spirit of the Lord (II Cor. 3:18).

Christian anthropology, then, with its theology of the Image, lays the groundwork for an ethical understanding of preaching as a work of love whose effectiveness lies in its ability to enkindle Christlike love in others. But beyond this, Christian anthropology prepares for a doxological understanding of preaching. We wrestle with texts, craft our sermons, and tailor our diction in love for those who will hear our words and attempt to live according to them. "The listener is king," say the old preaching manuals. No, he isn't, God is. No matter how crafted for human consumption, all sermons are ultimately addressed to God, whose word of love both invites and enables response. Paradoxically, the measure in which the sermon finds human ears and works love in situations of human suffering and unhappiness is the precise measure in which God is glorified.

"WHO IS SUFFICIENT FOR THESE THINGS?"

Paul asks this question in II Corinthians 2:16 in the context of his reflections on ministry and preaching. If we are to be more than "peddlers of God's word," as Paul branded his opponents, we need to utilize the resources available to every Christian man or woman. These include baptism, the community of the past, the brothers and sisters of today's church, the Scriptures, prayer, and the Holy Spirit.

Baptism. Nothing speaks more directly to the self's identity problems than baptism. Theological students and ministers who are struggling with professional or pastoral identity problems would do well to go behind the role, the mask, the *persona*, in order to discover the child of God in all its pure and uncomplicated reliance on the

Father. In baptism, the self without properties becomes a relational person who will never exist outside the life of the Father, the Son, and the Holy Spirit into whose name he or she has been baptized. At his own baptism Jesus emerged from the Jordan waters with a fuller measure of identity than when he entered them. At our baptisms too, we hear the voice say, "You are my beloved son; you are my beloved daughter." As the gateway to the church, baptism creates family or community for the Christian; at no time will the preacher have a life that is severed or alienated from this divine creation of family. Even at prophetic moments when the preacher speaks against the church, he or she never loses baptismal identity or ceases to be family.

The Community of the Past. "We are like pigmies standing on the shoulders of giants," said Bernard of Chartres. "We see farther than they but only because we are standing on their shoulders." There is a sense in which every sermon is a new beginning: new exegesis, new life-situations, new people, new applications. But we do not re-invent this task of preaching every week in the privacy of our studies, nor its anguish, its imperfect form, or its occasionally glorious fruitions. We rejoice in a linear relationship with Christian preachers of all ages, including Chrysostom, Augustine, Bonaventure, Berthold of Ratisbon, Luther, Calvin, Wesley, Whitefield, Schleiermacher, Robertson, Spurgeon, the Beechers, Brooks, Fosdick, Barth, Thurman, Thielicke, our family pastors, college chaplains, our fathers and mothers, and a galaxy of others upon whose shoulders we gratefully stand.

The Brothers and Sisters. As a young pastor I did not understand why my colleagues were so eager to attend jurisdictional meetings and conferences. With their inconsequential business agendas and unexciting programs, they seemed a waste of time. I soon discovered that their attraction had less to do with professional development than with the spiritual growth engendered by fellowship, worship, and preaching. One does not have to identify with the fictional prophet Brand to experience the loneliness and isolation of the Christian ministry. I suspect that the rate of ministerial mobility approaches that of the rest of the population, and I know that once beyond the well-defined role awaiting the new pastor, he or (especially) she finds real entry into the community to be a long and lonely process which yields little in the way of spiritual enrichment. The linear church must be complemented by the familial church, so that the minister also can be nurtured through experiences of worship over which he does not preside, and find sustenance in those rare instances when she is congregation to the preached word. This is how it is for men and women in ministry:

> Behold, how good and pleasant it is
> when brothers dwell in unity!
> It is like the precious oil upon the head,
> running down upon the beard, upon the beard of Aaron,
> running down on the collar of his robes! (Ps. 133:1-2).

The Scriptures. The Bible is the source of preaching and the sustainer of preachers. Before anyone can preach a biblical sermon, that person must have encountered Christ through the Bible. This paragraph takes into account the special sin of the student of the Bible, whether seminarian or clergy, which is searching the Scripture for information, data, theological support, or sermon material. There is nothing inherently good about reading the Bible unless one is encountering God in it. The pastor needs preparation for sermon preparation, that is, a time of meditative Bible reading before the work of exegesis begins. For one involved in weekly sermon preparation, the hours of meditative Bible study are repaid by God with a richness and depth of insight not available from commentaries or pulpit helps.

Prayer. Prayer is a response to the Word of God. Through Scripture and the sacraments God addresses his people; in prayer his people respond and enter into dialogue with him. When responding to the written word of God's goodness, the preacher may shape a prayer around the text for the day, articulating its central thought and thanking God for his wisdom revealed in it. The preacher may then pray for others, especially for those to whom he or she will bear witness, naming them and lifting up their needs before God. Next, the preacher must find words of prayer for those anxious and nervous feelings of which he or she is most ashamed. In the pulpit, the words of the psalmist are always appropriate:

> Let the words of my mouth, and the meditation
> of my heart, be acceptable in thy sight, O Lord,
> my strength, and my redeemer (Ps. 19:14 KJV).

After the sermon, the preacher gives thanks once again for the inestimable privilege of preaching. If it is the Word of God that has been proclaimed, said Luther, the preacher need not ask for forgiveness.

The Holy Spirit. The Spirit is the Seal of Christ who brings all things to remembrance. Helmut Thielicke observes that when Peter spoke on Pentecost his hearers were cut to the heart, for what was past had been made present tense, "today," for them. Thielicke goes on to call the Spirit the great Hermeneut whose work of spanning the distance between God and humankind serves as a protest against the divorce of subject and object.[19] By calling all things to remembrance, the Spirit creates the "understanding" for which the philosophers of hermeneutics search.

> For the Spirit searches everything, even the depths of God. For what person knows a man's thoughts except the spirit of the man which is in him? So also no one comprehends the thoughts of God except the Spirit of God. Now we have received not the spirit of the world, but the Spirit which is from God, that we might understand the gifts bestowed on us by God. And we impart this in words not taught by human wisdom but taught by the Spirit, interpreting spiritual truths to those who possess the Spirit (I Cor. 2:10*b*-13).

While we take pride in our knowledge of the human situation, by which knowledge we expect to make our sermons more accurate and effective, the Holy Spirit knows the interior contours of *God*. More than that, he is willing to call the Christ to our remembrance, to soothe our anxieties, to shape his words to our mouth no less carefully than Yahweh touched the lips of Isaiah or promised to "be with" Moses' mouth, all to this end: that preachers might speak, congregations might hear and believe, that God's will might be done on earth among all people, and, finally, that his name might be glorified forever.

NOTES

CHAPTER I: PREACHING AS THEOLOGY

1. Rudolf Bohren, *Preaching and Community*, trans. David E. Green (Richmond: John Knox Press, 1965), pp. 79-80.
2. Gerhard von Rad, *Biblical Interpretations in Preaching*, trans. John E. Steely (Nashville: Abingdon, 1977), p. 12. In addition to von Rad, several Old Testament scholars have attempted to close the gap between textual study and preaching: Foster McCurley, Jr., *Proclaiming the Promise* (Philadelphia, Fortress Press, 1974); Elizabeth Achtemeier, *The Old Testament and the Proclamation of the Gospel* (Philadelphia: The Westminster Press, 1973); Claus Westermann, ed., *Essays on Old Testament Hermeneutics*, trans. James Luther Mays (Richmond: John Knox Press, 1963). Among American New Testament scholars the work has just begun: Leander Keck, *The Bible in the Pulpit* (Nashville: Abingdon, 1978); D. Moody Smith, *Interpreting the Gospels for Preaching* (Philadelphia: Fortress Press, 1980).
3. Gerhard Ebeling, *Word and Faith*, trans. James W. Leitch (Philadelphia: Fortress Press, 1963), p. 424.
4. Walter Wink, "How I Have Been Snagged by the Seat of My Pants While Reading the Bible," *The Christian Century* (September 24, 1975), 816. Warnings against academic theology severed from pastoral concerns have appeared in sources as diverse as Thomas C. Oden, *Agenda for Theology* (San Francisco: Harper & Row, 1979), pp. 22-26, 74-78; E. L. Mascall, *Theology and the Gospel of Christ* (London: S.P.C.K., 1977), pp. 15-16; Henry Mitchell, *The Recovery of Preaching* (New York: Harper & Row, 1977), pp. 6-7.
5. Robert Browne, *The Ministry of the Word* (Philadelphia: Fortress Press, 1976), p. 34.
6. I am indebted to the spirit of Paul Tillich's introduction to his *Systematic Theology* vol. I (University of Chicago Press, 1951), pp. 28-68.
7. Ebeling, *Word and Faith*, p. 424.

8. Karl Barth, *Church Dogmatics*, vol. I, pt. 1, trans. G. T. Thomson (New York: Charles Scribner's Sons, 1936), pp. 2-3, 56.

9. Heinrich Ott, *Theology and Preaching*, trans. Harold Knight (Philadelphia: The Westminster Press, 1961), p. 23.

10. Gerhard Ebeling, *Theology and Proclamation*, trans. John Riches (Philadelphia: Fortress Press, 1966), p. 20.

11. P. T. Forsyth, *Positive Preaching and Modern Mind* (New York: Armstrong, 1905), p. 205.

12. *Apology of the Augsburg Confession*, IV, 2-3. Cf. Hermann Diem, "Der Theologie zwischen Text und Predigt," in *Aufgabe der Predigt*, ed. Gert Hummel (Darmstadt: Wissenschaftliche Buchgesellschaft, 1971), pp. 281-82.

13. Tillich, *Systematic Theology*, vol. I, p. 61.

14. Ernst Fuchs, *Hermeneutik* (Bad Cannstatt: Müllerschon, 1958), p. 99. Cf. Ott, p. 20. Note the section "Verkündigung an die Welt," in *Wort in Welt*, ed. by Karl Rahner and Bernhard Häring (Bergen-Enkheim bei Frankfurt/M.: Gerhard Kaffke, 1968), pp. 285-382.

15. Yngve Brilioth, *A Brief History of Preaching*, trans. Karl E. Mattson (Philadelphia: Fortress Press, 1965), pp. 161-70 *et passim*.

16. *The Smalcald Articles*, Part III, Art. IV.

17. From the *Church Postil*, "The Gospel for the Festival of the Epiphany," trans. S. P. Hebart, *Luther's Works*, vol. 52, ed. Hans. J. Hillerbrand (Philadelphia: Fortress Press, 1974), p. 206.

18. Frederick E. Crowe, *Theology of the Christian Word* (New York: Paulist Press, 1978), p. 53.

19. Domenico Grasso, *Proclaiming God's Message* (South Bend: Notre Dame University Press, 1965), p. 244. Cf. Brilioth, p. 70.

20. Geoffrey Wainwright, *Doxology: The Praise of God in Worship, Doctrine and Life* (New York: Oxford University Press, 1980).

21. Mascall, *Theology and the Gospel of Christ*, p. 24.

22. Friedrich Schleiermacher, *Brief Outline of the Study of Theology*, trans. William Farrer (Edinburgh: T. & T. Clark, 1850; reprinted by The American Theological Library Association, Lexington, Kentucky, 1963), p. 97. Schleiermacher's italics omitted.

23. Tillich, *Systematic Theology*, vol. I, p. 58.

CHAPTER II: *RESURREXIT:* POWER TO PREACH

1. Some scholars understand the resurrection as an appendix to the life of Jesus, with the result that his true authority derives from his earthly ministry and teaching. In this group Wolfhart Pannenberg includes Ebeling, Bornkamm, Käsemann, and Tillich. For Pannenberg's own position see *Jesus—God and Man*, 2nd ed., trans. Lewis Wilkins and Duane Priebe (Philadelphia: The Westminster Press, 1977), pp. 108-11.

2. Willi Marxsen, *The Resurrection of Jesus of Nazareth*, trans. Margaret Kohl (Philadelphia: Fortress Press, 1970), p. 128.

3. Jürgen Moltmann, *Theology of Hope*, trans. James Leitch (New York: Harper & Row, 1967), p. 173.

4. Marxsen, *Resurrection of Jesus of Nazareth*, p. 147.

5. Moltmann, *Theology of Hope*, p. 188 (my italics).
6. Jürgen Moltmann, *The Crucified God*, trans. R. A. Wilson and John Bowden (New York: Harper & Row, 1974), p. 174.
7. Moltmann, *Theology of Hope*, pp. 180-81. On this distinction see my article, "An Old/New Theology of History," *The Christian Century* (March 13, 1974), 289.
8. Moltmann is dialoguing with Marx's definition of religion as "the *expression* of real distress and the *protest* against real distress" in "Toward a Political Hermeneutics of the Gospel," *New Theology No. 6*, ed. Martin E. Marty and Dean Peerman (London: Macmillan & Co., 1969), p. 69.
9. *Tertullian's Treatise on the Resurrection*, ed. & trans. Ernest Evans (London: S.P.C.K., 1960), ch. 6, 11. 10-12, p. 19.
10. Pierre Teilhard de Chardin, *Hymn of the Universe*, trans. Gerald Vann (New York: Harper & Row, 1961), pp. 65-67 (italics omitted).
11. Rudolf Bultmann, *Theology of the New Testament*, vol. I, trans. Kendrick Grobel (London: SCM Press, 1952), pp. 293-94.
12. Indispensable to this discussion are: Stephen Crites, "The Narrative Quality of Experience," *Journal of the American Academy of Religion*, vol. 39, no. 3 (September 1971), 291-311; James B. Wiggins, ed., *Religion as Story* (New York: Harper & Row, 1975); and the bibliography assembled by Sallie McFague in the 1977 issue of *Homiletic*.
13. *De catechizandis rudibus*, 3:5; 6:10, quoted in Grasso, pp. 115-16.
14. Amos Wilder, *Early Christian Rhetoric* (Cambridge: Harvard University Press, 1971 reissue), pp. 58, 66.
15. Robert Funk, *Language, Hermeneutic, and Word of God* (New York: Harper & Row, 1966), p. 18.
16. Eugen Rosenstock-Huessy, *Speech and Reality* (Norwich, Vt.: Argo Books, 1970), p. 50.
17. Sam Keen, *To a Dancing God* (New York: Harper & Row, 1970), p. 99.
18. *A Service of Death and Resurrection*, Supplemental Worship Resources 7 (Nashville: Abingdon, 1979), p. 13.
19. This is Carl Michalson's observation in *The Hinge of History* (New York: Charles Scribner's Sons, 1959), p. 210.
20. Martin Luther, *Werke*, Weimar Edition, vol. 34, I, p. 318, 11. 15-16. Cf. Gustaf Wingren, *The Living Word*, trans. Victor Pogue (Philadelphia: Muhlenberg, 1960), p. 68. The sense of Luther's remarks on John 20 is echoed in Bultmann's "Reply" in *The Theology of Rudolf Bultmann*, ed. Charles W. Kegley (New York: Harper & Row), pp. 260-61.

CHAPTER III: HOW LAW AND GOSPEL WORK IN PREACHING

1. Paul Tillich, *Theology of Culture*, ed. Robert C. Kimball (New York: Oxford University Press, 1959), pp. 203-4; and *Systematic Theology*, vol. II, pp. 44-47. An important book in this area is Herman Stuempfle, *Preaching Law and Gospel* (Philadelphia: Fortress Press, 1978), p. 24.
2. Stuempfle, *Preaching Law and Gospel*, p. 25.
3. *Lectures on Romans*, trans. Jacob A. O. Preus, *Luther's Works*, vol. 25, ed. Hilton Oswald, p. 299.

꒐ 1757

4. For example, Kyle Haselden, *The Urgency of Preaching* (New York: Harper & Row, 1963); Peril, Promise, Alterant (pp. 52-65); Ott, *Theology and Preaching*: Wretchedness, Redemption, Gratitude (p. 53); Richard Caemmerer, *Preaching for the Church* (St. Louis: Concordia Publishing House, 1959): Goal, Malady, Means (pp. 15-45); Milton Crum, Jr., *Manual on Preaching* (Valley Forge, Pa.: Judson Press, 1977): Symptomatic behavior, Root cause, Resulting consequences, Gospel content, New results (pp. 20-21).

5. Karl Barth, "Gospel and Law," in *Community, State, and Church*, no trans. given (Garden City, N.Y.: Doubleday-Anchor, 1960), p. 80.

6. Quoted in Wainwright, *Doxology*, p. 273.

7. Merton P. Strommen, *et al.*, *A Study of Generations* (Minneapolis: Augsburg Publishing House, 1972), p. 132.

8. Werner Kümmel, *Römer 7 und das Bild des Menschen im Neuen Testament* (Munich: Chr. Kaiser, 1974), pp. 87, 186. Rudolf Bultmann, "Romans 7 and the Anthropology of Paul," in *Existence and Faith*, trans. Schubert Ogden (Cleveland: Meridian Books, 1960), p. 147.

9. See St. Augustine, *The Retractions*, chap. 23, trans. Mary Inez Bogan, *The Fathers of the Church*, vol. 60 (Washington, D.C.: The Catholic University Press, 1968), p. 103; Luther; *Lectures on Romans*, p. 327; John Calvin, *Commentaries on . . . Romans*, trans. John Owen (Grand Rapids: Eerdmans Publishing Co., 1948), pp. 261-63; Karl Barth, *The Epistle to the Romans*, trans. Edwyn Hoskyns (London: Oxford University Press, 1933), p. 270; Anders Nygren, *Commentary on Romans*, trans. Carl Rasmussen (Philadelphia: Fortress Press, 1949), pp. 284-92.

10. Barth, "Gospel and Law," in *Community, State, and Church*, pp. 71-100; Werner Elert, *Law and Gospel*, trans. Edward Schroeder (Philadelphia: Fortress Press, 1967); Helmut Thielicke, *The Evangelical Faith*, vol. II, trans. and ed. Geoffrey W. Bromiley (Grand Rapids: Eerdmans Publishing Co., 1977), pp. 184-242; Gerhard O. Forde, *The Law-Gospel Debate* (Minneapolis: Augsburg Press, 1969), pp. 137-74.

11. W. D. Davies, *Invitation to the New Testament* (Garden City, N.Y.: Doubleday-Anchor), pp. 39-49.

12. Reuel Howe, *Partners in Preaching* (New York: The Seabury Press, 1967), pp. 27-28.

13. Jefferson adds, "I have performed this operation for my own use, by cutting verse by verse out of the printed book. . . . " *The Adams-Jefferson Letters*, vol. II, ed. Lester J. Cappon (Chapel Hill: University of North Carolina Press, 1959), p. 384.

14. Two specimens of moralistic preaching may be found in James W. Cox, ed., *The Twentieth-Century Pulpit* (Nashville: Abingdon, 1978). They are "Power Over All Your Difficulties" by Norman Vincent Peale (pp. 167-74) and "Bearing His Reproach" by W. E. Sangster (pp. 180-87). There are others. In the same volume, George Buttrick, "Is It the Golden Rule?" meets the issue of moralism head-on and deals with it successfully (pp. 30-35).

15. Thielicke, *The Evangelical Faith*, vol. II, p. 195.

16. Dietrich Bonhoeffer, "Finkenwalde Lectures on Homiletics," in Clyde E. Fant, *Bonhoeffer: Worldly Preaching* (New York: Thomas Nelson, 1975), p. 180.

CHAPTER IV: PREACHING AS THE WORD OF GOD

1. Walter Ong, *The Presence of the Word* (New Haven: Yale University Press, 1967); *Interfaces of the Word* (Ithaca, N.Y.: Cornell University Press, 1977).
2. Ong, *Interfaces of the Word*, p. 18.
3. Birger Gerhardsson, *Memory and Manuscript*, trans. Eric J. Sharpe, Acta Seminarii Neotestamentici Upsaliensis, XXII (Uppsala, Sweden: Gleerup, 1961), p. 163. His remarks on orality contribute to his persuasive argument for the reliability of the New Testament witnesses based on his recor struction of the organized use of memory and oral transmission in the early church (cf. pp. 244-45, 325-34, *et passim*).
4. Ong, *The Presence of the Word*, pp. 66-69.
5. Ibid., pp. 111-12. See "*Maranatha*: Death and Life in the Text of the Book," in *Interfaces of the Word*, pp. 230-71.
6. Ibid., pp. 166-67.
7. Rosenstock-Huessy, *Speech and Reality*, p. 145.
8. Ibid., p. 137.
9. Wilder, *Early Christian Rhetoric*, p. 13.
10. Luther, *Werke*, Weimar Ed., vol. 49, p. 360, 1. 28; vol. 37, p. 202, 11. 14-22, quoted in Wingren, p. 64. Barth has collected many of Luther's sayings on oral preaching in *Church Dogmatics*, vol. I, pt. 1, pp. 137-40.
11. See the articles related to *lego* and *logos* by A. Debrunner, H. Kleinknecht, O. Procksch, and G. Kittel in Gerhard Kittel, ed., *Theological Dictionary of the New Testament*, vol. IV, trans. Geoffrey Bromiley (Grand Rapids: Eerdmans Publishing Co., 1967); and James Barr's critique, *The Semantics of Biblical Language* (London: Oxford University Press, 1961), pp. 129-39; see also Rudolf Bultmann, "The Concept of the Word of God in the New Testament," in *Faith and Understanding*, vol. I, ed. Robert Funk, trans. Louise Smith (New York: Harper & Row, 1969), pp. 286-312; also, Jerome Murphy-O'Connor, *Paul on Preaching* (New York: Sheed & Ward, 1963), pp. 147-49 *et passim*. On performative discourse see J. L. Austin, "Performative-Constative," in *The Philosophy of Language*, ed. J. R. Searle (London: Oxford University Press, 1971), pp. 13-22; and on "the hunger for names" note Ernst Cassirer, *An Essay on Man* (Garden City: Doubleday, 1954), pp. 170-71.
12. Wilder, *Early Christian Rhetoric*, p. 10.
13. Bultmann, *Faith and Understanding*, vol. I, p. 308.
14. T. S. Eliot, "Gerontion," *Selected Poems* (London: Faber & Faber, 1961).
15. See Bohren, *Preaching and Community*, p. 98.
16. Barth, *Church Dogmatics* vol. I, pt. 1, p. 151; Bonhoeffer, *Worldly Preaching*, p. 127.
17. Keck, *The Bible in the Pulpit*, p. 31.
18. Ernest Best speaks of the Scriptures as "freezings," "precipitates," and "crystallizations" in *From Text to Sermon* (Atlanta: John Knox Press, 1978), pp. 11-32.
19. Barth, *Church Dogmatics*, vol. I, pt. 2, p. 755.
20. Ibid., pt. 1, p. 136.
21. See Ong, *Interfaces of the Word*, pp. 104, 114; and Mitchell, *The Recovery of Preaching*, pp. 74-95.

22. Rosenstock-Huessy, *Speech and Reality*, p. 162. Augustine often commented on the fleeting nature of the preached word and contrasted it to the eternal Word, God himself. See the *Tractates on the Gospel of John*, I, chap. 8, trans. John Gibb and James Innes, *Nicene and Post Nicene Fathers*, First Series, ed. Philip Schaff, vol. 7 (New York: Christian Literature, 1888).
23. Rosenstock-Huessy, *Speech and Reality*, pp. 179-80.

CHAPTER V: CHRISTIAN ANTHROPOLOGY AND THE POSSIBILITY OF PREACHING

1. Blaise Pascal, *Pensées*, trans. W. F. Trotter (New York: E. P. Dutton, 1958), sect. VII, 434.
2. Henrik Ibsen, *Brand*, trans. Michael Meyer (London: Rupert Hart-Davis, 1960), Act I, p. 27.
3. Wilder, *Early Christian Rhetoric*, p. 2.
4. See P. Albert Duhamel, "The Function of Rhetoric as Effective Expression," in *The Province of Rhetoric*, ed. Joseph Schwartz and John Rycenga (New York: Ronald Press, 1965), pp. 44-46.
5. I have expanded on this in *Marx and Teilhard: Two Ways to the New Humanity* (Maryknoll, N.Y.: Orbis Books, 1979), pp. 19-20.
6. Jürgen Moltmann, *Man*, trans. John Sturdy (Philadelphia: Fortress Press, 1974), p. 12.
7. Quoted in Ernest Becker, *The Denial of Death* (New York: The Free Press, 1973), xiv.
8. Funk, *Language, Hermeneutic, and Word of God*, p. 9.
9. Tillich, *Systematic Theology*, vol. II, p. 60.
10. Hans-Georg Gadamer, *Truth and Method*, trans. not given (New York: The Seabury Press, 1975), pp. 272-74. A valuable introduction to philosophical hermeneutics is Richard E. Palmer, *Hermeneutics* (Evanston: Ill. Northwestern University Press, 1969).
11. R. G. Collingwood, *The Idea of History* (London: Oxford University Press, 1956), pp. 282-83.
12. Wolfhart Pannenberg, *Basic Questions in Theology*, vol. I, trans. George H. Kehm (Philadelphia: Fortress Press, 1970), pp. 11-12.
13. See Barth, *Church Dogmatics*, vol. I, pt. 1, pp. 190-91.
14. Quoted in James M. Robinson and John B. Cobb, Jr., *The New Hermeneutic, New Frontiers in Theology*, vol. II (New York: Harper & Row, 1964), p. 25.
15. Funk, *Language, Hermeneutic, and Word of God*, p. 7.
16. The discussion of the Image of God closely follows my argument in *Marx and Teilhard*, pp. 71-73.
17. This is the thesis of Emil Brunner's influential anthropology, *Man in Revolt*, trans. Olive Wyon (Philadelphia: The Westminster Press, orig. issued 1939).
18. Aquinas, *Summa Theologiae*, I, q. 93, a. 8 (italics omitted).
19. Thielicke, *The Evangelical Faith*, vol. I, pp. 130-33.

INDEX OF SUBJECTS

INDEX OF BIBLICAL REFERENCES